Backstage Iditarod

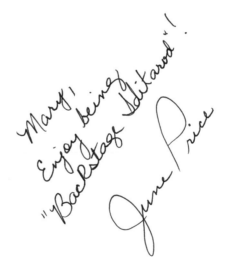

Mary!
Enjoy being Iditarod!
"Backstage Iditarod"!
June Price

June Price

#91

Cover Photographer: Karen Ramstead
Back Cover Photographer: Donna Quante
Graphics Consultant: Jan DeNapoli
Editors: Helen Hegener, Heather Walls

Photographers: Brenda Borden, www.duesouthphoto.com
Jan DeNapoli, www.muzzysplace.net
Karen Ramstead, www.northwapiti.com
Mary Dillingham, http://home.gci.net/~sleddog/
Donna Quante, www.huskyproductions.net
Betty Walden
All other photos by the author

Library of Congress Control Number: 2007905123

ISBN 10: 0-9795828-4-9
ISBN 13: 978-0-9795828-4-4

Printed in the United States of America

Productions
Sunhusky Productions
Wasilla, AK 99654
Orders: www.sunhuskyproductions.com

Acknowledgements

To my Iditarod Family, thank you. Without you, this book wouldn't exist. Each of you has contributed to this book in unique and special ways. Enjoy "your" book.

Ed Iten dogs. Photo: Jan DeNapoli, www.muzzysplace.net

Contents

Lance Mackey, 2007 Champion, with leaders Larry and Lippy.
Photo: Brenda Borden, www.duesouthphoto.com

Chapter 1

Lance Mackey, 2007:
A Dream, a Vision, and Lucky #13

Lance Mackey on the way to the starting line of Iditarod 2007.

"I owe it all to an incredible dog team," declares Lance Mackey. "It was an honor to see the *Anchorage Daily News* acknowledging their accomplishment."

The Anchorage paper did a brief profile on the Mackey dogs, noting the personality and contributions of each. The contribution of the dogs loomed large in Mackey's mind.

In 2006, while approaching Nome in 10th place, Mackey showed this trait to the world. The man who refused to give into tears during his bout with cancer stopped five miles short of the Burled Arch to take one last moment alone with his dogs. For reasons that will probably never be understood by those of us who aren't mushers, the finish of the race can be an emotional one.

Many mushers reveal the urge to turn around so the moment doesn't have to end. Mackey had one of those moments. Stopping on the ice, he took some quiet time with his dogs, telling them, "We did it."

Lance Mackey under the Burled Arch with leaders Larry, left, and Lippy.
Photo: Brenda Borden, www.duesouthphoto.com

"I just kinda lived up to my dogs' expectations of me," Mackey said in 2007, once again acknowledging the role of the dogs. He'd gone into the Yukon Quest only weeks before planning to run two different teams in the two races. Although the Quest victory certainly wasn't an easy one for Mackey, he wasn't pressed to the degree he'd expected, which lead to him running essentially the same dog team in both races. And, to answer the question most frequently asked at race time, thirteen of his Quest dogs ran the Iditarod with him.

"I had hopes, a dream, and a vision," he said. "I was racing myself, not anyone else in particular."

Taking one day at a time seemed to be his motto. Noting that he has been underestimated by some, Mackey emphasized that he didn't get wrapped up in what everyone else was doing, either before or during the race. He ran his own race.

"Some teams went by me early on in the Iditarod," he said, "making it look at times like I was tied to a tree." He flashed a grin. "I figured I'd see them again, tho', and I did." He paused, letting it sink in that he meant he'd passed the teams that blew past him earlier, teams that never saw anything but his back for the rest of the race.

While some have argued that Lance Mackey has been simply lucky victory-wise in the past, it's hard for anyone to argue that anymore. He might thrive on being seen as an underdog, but his skill and natural dog savvy deserve recognition. He's done what no musher before him thought possible, winning the two premiere long distance sled dog races in the same year. As four-time Iditarod Champion Jeff King quipped early in the race after watching Lance pass him on one runner, "It's not chance, it's Lance."

Mackey had his share of problems in both races, but his Iditarod experiences were magnified when he broke his sled in the Quest. As a result, he didn't send out a second sled in the Iditarod, a mistake he noted he'd never make again. 150 miles into the Iditarod, he broke a runner, just the beginning of his problems.

As a result, "I did the Gorge and the Burn on one runner." He had the option of waiting a day, perhaps more, for a sled to be flown out to him during this early stage of the race. He chose to continue on his broken sled.

"It wasn't the most fun I've ever had," Mackey deadpanned, "but it was certainly memorable."

He recalls following four-time champion Martin Buser along one stretch of trail, getting some amusement watching Buser, on two good runners, take a spill. "Of course, while I was chuckling, I fell over myself," he notes with a sigh. Such is life on the Iditarod Trail, although Mackey took obvious pride in remembering passing previous champion Buser on one runner.

At Rohn, a long-time checker offered Mackey the use of some old skis. Such help is allowed when it's freely available to all.

"The MacGyver in me came out," laughed Mackey. Fashioning the old skis into runners, he was able to make it up the trail. "It wasn't pretty, but it worked."

Probably feeling as if he were inside a giant pinball machine, he hit tussock after tussock, was tossed over the handlebars, and dragged, dirt in his mouth instead of snow, in general just miserable. At one point he vowed to rip the makeshift runners off the sled as he was thinking it'd been easier with just one runner. But he didn't have to rip them off; they broke, too.

Alaska Amber Brewing Company came to his rescue. Remember, Mackey hadn't shipped out a second sled. Alaska Amber chartered a plane and flew a sled to him in McGrath.

While having an unbroken sled certainly helped, it wasn't easy, even then. His dogs picked up a virus and he felt the need to back off from the pace. "At that point, I figured I wasn't going to win the race," he admitted, but he was determined to finish with happy, healthy dogs. He credits the vets with making it possible to continue and eventually win the race.

Taking his 24 hour layover in Iditarod, he cited the teamwork that came into play with a former neighbor, Paul Gebhardt. Both had planned on going further, but the trail did not allow that. There was still no snow and it was rough, even on two runners.

By that point, "there was no room for mistakes," said Mackey, "absolutely none."

Working together, Mackey and Gebhardt were able to make up time on then front runners Buser and King, with Zach Steer right on their heels.

The rest, as they say, is history. Mackey's exuberant run up Front Street in Nome will long be remembered.

Photo: Brenda Borden, duesouthphotos.com

Chas St. George, the Iditarod's public relations director, noted that "Lance was up and down the chute, thanking everyone, embracing the victory, talking to the fans, pulling them into the moment."

As he ran, barely escaping being tackled and knocked to the ground by younger brother Jason, Mackey pointed to the #13 bib adorning his chest. Improbable as it might seem, he'd done exactly what he set out to do: win the Iditarod on his sixth try, wearing the same number his father Dick

Mackey and brother Rick had worn during their victories, both also on their sixth Iditarod.

"I owe it all to the dogs," Mackey declares. "I'm not sure if this (the back-to-back victories in the Quest and Iditarod) can ever be duplicated, but I hope if it is, it's me that does it."

Since then, of course, life has changed for Lance Mackey. He's been invited to Las Vegas and Norway and places in-between. He's no longer total master of his own schedule and he counts on friends to help manage his time. As this book went to press, he'd just received word of his nomination for an ESPY Award as Best Outdoor Athlete. ESPN was to fly him to Hollywood for the ceremony where he'd play golf with the likes of Tiger Woods. Although he didn't win his category, he enjoyed the experience.

Asked about his golf game at the Iditarod's volunteer picnic in the summer of 2007, where he posed for photos with Alaskan Governor Sarah Palin, Mackey laughed. "I've played golf three times in my life," he admitted "and two of 'em were this week."

He didn't seem terribly concerned. People who know Lance well will tell you, 'what you see is what you get.' This is the real Lance Mackey. Playing golf with Tiger Woods and hanging out in Hollywood is of less interest to him than finishing his rounds of public appearances on behalf of his sport and getting back to his dog lot this fall. Turn the topic to dogs, however, and he becomes energized.

"I want people to know that I love life and I love my dogs," he declared without hesitation when asked how he'd like to be remembered.

Speaking for the little guy, Mackey went on to note that the sheer fact he was standing there as a dual Iditarod and Yukon Quest Champion was proof positive that someone with "a beat up truck, devotion and dedication to their dogs, and a love of the sport" could succeed.

From this, Iditarod dreams are kindled.

Larry, 2007 Golden Harness winner, and Lance Mackey
Photo: Brenda Borden, www.duesouthphoto.com

Mitch Seavey's leaders. Photo: Jan DeNapoli, www.muzzysplace.net

Chapter 2

The Cost of a Dream

Photo by Donna Quante, www.huskyproductions.net

Martin Buser estimated in 2005 that each dog in his kennel costs him $1.50 per day. That's per day, every day of the year, whether they're running on the team or not, whether there is snow on the ground or not.

Do the basic math. Assume you have 25 dogs competing to be on your Iditarod team. That $1.50 becomes $37.50 a day. Don't stop there, however. $37.50 a day suddenly becomes more than $1,125 per month and that is if nothing extra is needed. $1,125 per month turns into over $13,500 per year. Most Iditarod kennels have more than 25 dogs, of course.

That basic cost does not include extras like supplements, special foods, unexpected vet bills, transportation and everything else. It's easy to forget this element of regular expense that eats away at the bank account when Iditarod dreams capture the imagination.

In Buser's opinion, this is one of the most misunderstood aspects of the sport. "It's a business and it's expensive. Money is doled out on a daily basis and you're often not aware of how much it is genuinely costing you until it's too late."

The dogs are the biggest expense. Solid leaders can cost upwards of $2,500. In addition, few mushers use the same sled more than two years in a row. The wear and tear of the trail tends to batter sleds and few mushers want to hazard the likes of Happy River with a weakened sled. Not only does their safety depend on it, so does the well-being of the dogs pulling it.

Thus, should you decide to run the Iditarod, plan on spending an average of $2,500 for a sled and sled bag. Most mushers ship out at least one additional sled, too, which costs around $400 just to ship. And, don't forget, the plastic on the runners has to be changed frequently. Fifteen extra sets of sled plastic will set you back around $400.

The sled bag functions as your suitcase. Anything you want or need on the trail must go in there or in your drop bags, bags of supplies shipped to checkpoints. The Iditarod Trail Committee (ITC) specifies a select list of mandatory items. Let's take a look at them first.

You must have a "proper cold weather sleeping bag weighing a minimum of five pounds." It could run you $300 but the higher the quality, the better. Your life may depend on it. Temperatures during the Iditarod often dip into the -40° range or below.

The second item listed is one you don't hear much about, an axe. The head must weigh a minimum of 1.75 lbs, with a handle at least 22 inches long. This is useful if you have to chop your way out from under a downed tree or gather firewood. It may also be needed to field dress a moose or other game that one might have to kill to protect the team. Prices on the Cabela's website range from a low of about $30 up to around $45.

Snowshoes with bindings, each at least 252 square inches in size, are next on the list. Snowshoes range from "ol' fashioned" wooden ones, about $95 per pair, to lighter weight aluminum ones with high tech bindings for about $275 per pair.

The next item listed is free to the musher, but priceless to fans. At their pre-race meeting just days before the race begins, one of the tasks that mushers face is that of signing a set of promotional cache envelopes. The design changes each year. This is to commemorate the race's roots in the original serum run of 1925, as well as to pay tribute to Alaska's historic mail teams.

Musher Bill Borden helps auction off trail cachets at the Nome Finisher's Banquet not long after finishing Iditarod 2002. The design that year was by his wife, Brenda Borden, who supplied this photo. www.duesouthphoto.com

Used booties, freshly washed for re-use.

"Eight booties for each dog in the sled or in use," is next. Most mushers package the required number of booties, tape the bag shut, and never open it, thus ensuring they always have the required number available. The average cost of a bootie is $1.00, although they can be considerably cheaper if you're able to make your own. Mushers calculate that they need an average of 1,500 booties. Not all will go into the sled bag; many will be shipped out in drop bags, but this is a subtle and often overlooked expense. Booties are also popular fan souvenirs, so extras are often added.

The veterinarian notebook is provided by the Iditarod Trail Committee and must be presented to the veterinarian at each checkpoint. The notebook is pocket sized and designed to allow use in wind, rain or snow without the writing becoming smeared. "Vet books will be signed by a veterinarian," read the 2008 rules, "or in the absence of a veterinarian may be signed by a designated race official. The musher will also sign the vet book." These are collected from the mushers at the end of the race but returned to them later for their own records.

One of the most used items in the sled will be the "operational cooker and pot capable of boiling at least three gallons of water at a time." The type most used seems to average $100 new, which includes both the cooker and handled bucket for water. Remember, you'll need bowls and a dipper for the dogs, too!

In addition, "an adequate amount of fuel to bring three gallons of water to a boil" is required. The Iditarod supplies fuel for the mushers at checkpoints but the requirement is to carry three or four bottles at $.50 to $1.00 per bottle. Another mandatory item is a "cable gang line or cable tie out capable of securing dog team."

Emergency dogfood must also be carried when leaving a checkpoint. This is in addition to that which would normally be carried "for routine feeding and snacking."

These mandatory items, of course, make up just a fraction of the gear and supplies needed, but don't forget they need to get the dogs home from Nome, too. Allow approximately $600 for that process, plus the cost of the shipping crates and getting them to Nome.

The Iditarod Trail Committee requires a deposit of $200 up front as a deposit toward any dog care needed beyond the norm. This is in addition to the (2008) entry fee of $3,000.

Rookie mushers face an obstacle that veterans don't have to face. They have to qualify for the Iditarod, completing two sanctioned qualifying races that total 500 miles. Entry fees vary. For instance, the entry fee for the Knik 200 was $200 in 2006, while the Klondike entry fee was set at $350. This doesn't take into consideration the travel time and expense of travel. North American mushers face high fuel prices, but imagine the cost facing mushers shipping dogs from overseas. Even Alaskan mushers face this issue as many live where there isn't a road system. And all rookies must attend a mandatory rookie meeting the first weekend of December, adding additional travel costs.

The differences don't stop there. Visit some kennels and the mushers can throw open a door and show you everything they'll need, neatly stacked and labeled, including a new set of matching harnesses. Harnesses cost an average of $25-30 each, depending upon the style. Visit rookie Joe Musher's kennel, however, and you may find him scrambling to find an unchewed harness, let alone one that's color coordinated.

Martin Buser's dog truck looks fresh off the showroom floor. Visit even some veteran back of the packers, however, and they can only dream of such things. Their trucks often sport rust, not full color promo photos, with duct tape holding things together. There's no spare cash for repairs. Mushers have missed races for this reason. 2007 Champion Lance Mackey, known for his perpetual truck problems, even came close to missing a few starts that winter, making his 2007 Iditarod victory all the sweeter since it came with a brand new Anchorage-Dodge donated truck.

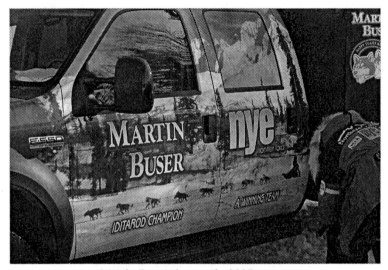

Martin Buser dog truck, 2007 restart

Drop bags are a huge commitment, both in time and money. They must be packed and delivered to a central point several weeks prior to the race. Every year, the ITC gets frantic calls from mushers saying their drop bags will be delayed due to vehicle problems. It would probably be fair to say mushers ship out an average of 1,600 pounds, which may be on the low end for most. They pay by the pound.

What's in those bags? First, there's dog and people food, of course. Generally, a mix of kibble and meat for the dogs is shipped, with tempting snacks for both dogs and humans included. In addition to the snacks and regular meals, kibble is often bagged in Zip-Lock® bags, each bag ready for water to be added later to tempt the dogs to drink enough baited water to stay hydrated. The kibble alone might cost up to $50 per fifty pound sack for a proven, top-of-the-line sled dog food, the meat another $600 or more.

What else might you find in a musher's drop bag? Plenty of work gloves, the cheap kind you can buy off the rack in almost any store. These are worn at checkpoints and during breaks. Many wear what might be deemed an Arctic Mitt while traveling, often made of fur with a fur lining for added warmth. Cost? About $100.

The proper clothing is vital. Ideally, if all goes well, mushers won't need anything but basic winter gear, plus a few changes of clothing, such as extra hats, mittens, socks, neck scarves, a warm shirt or perhaps a change of long underwear. Yet, to outfit yourself properly, the cost could be $600 or more. Boot liners are equally important, although they can be dried out and reused. Extras are nice to have as the opportunity and space to perform this simple task at most checkpoints is limited, and the alternative might be frostbite. So, add another, say, $40 per set for quality boot-liners which go into cold weather boots that can cost in the vicinity of $200 a pair.

On the trail, mushers depend on everything working, especially their headlamps ($135). While it's certainly possible to travel in the dark and, in fact, many prefer to do so, when light is needed it's usually vital. As a result, you'll often find at least one spare headlamp and not just extra bulbs ($6) but batteries. Lithium batteries are the ones of choice and they don't come cheap. They average $15 each.

What else? It'd probably be a safe hunch to figure on an ample supple of hand and foot warmers. These might total $50-100, depending on how cold their feet tend to get! Body heat wraps can warm the whole body. With the high-tech fabrics of today, not to mention Jeff King's recent heated handle bar, this is less of a concern than it was in the past, but it's a comforting thought to most to know they have some quick heat available if needed. These packets can be used to warm up batteries and extend battery life, too, as well as for the dogs, who might also be decked out in high-tech gear. Top quality dog coats cost about $50 apiece.

Somewhere in the sled bag will be an ample supply of such things as hooks, snaps, and "miscellaneous" items that may be vitally important at some point. Extreme cold can play havoc on metal, so extras are important. Cost? Well, it depends. If you're carrying lots of spare cash, perhaps not many need be carried as you can purchase such items at certain checkpoints. Still, the wise musher will have extras, often to the tune of $100 worth, along with the materials needed to repair a busted gangline or fix broken runners in the middle of nowhere.

By now it should be obvious that there is no one list of costs. Packing for the Iditarod race is an individual process, one that tends to result in at least one rookie musher who packed everything but the kitchen sink. Even then, they're likely to look on with envy at a checkpoint and wish they'd thought of packing a plastic kid's toboggan sled for hauling items from place to place at checkpoints. They'll wish they'd thought of picking up some plastic bottles or tubes to carry ointments in, or devised pockets in their sled bag to keep things handy like their vet book and regularly needed items. They'll wish they had some extra bottles of Algyval, at about $32 for slightly over six ounces, for doggie aches and pains. Most mushers will carry a gun capable of bringing down a moose. And don't forget the duct tape!

Rookies will watch and learn. It is little things that make a huge difference, lessons that are learned only from experience. The Iditarod is an expensive classroom, but one most mushers wouldn't trade for the world.

Nils Hahn works on his sled runners at Finger Lake Checkpoint, 2002

Aliy Zirkle flashes a smile at the summer picnic in 2007.

Chapter 3

Signing-Up:
Volunteer Picnic

Alaskan Governor Sarah Palin poses with 2007 Iditarod Champion Lance Mackey at the 2007 picnic.

Had you wandered into Iditarod Headquarters in Wasilla on the last Saturday in June, 2007, you might have been forgiven for thinking you'd stumbled into a political gathering. Alaska's Governor Sarah Palin was there, shaking hands, posing for photos, and even signing a few autographs.

If you took a closer look, however, you might have noticed something strange. While the Governor was certainly drawing a crowd, much of the audience was elsewhere. They were in search of mushers to sign autographs and pose for photos, not former mayor and Wasilla hometown-girl-made-good Sarah Palin.

This picnic is an Iditarod ritual of summer. Volunteers gather to be honored, while mushers gather to fill out paperwork and pay the entry fee for the next race. It's an interesting mix. You've got the likes of past champions Mitch Seavey and Martin Buser, while Buser's son Rohn was also on hand to enter the race for his rookie run, as were any number of Iditarod dreamers. Back of the pack mushers rub elbows at the sign-up table with not just these champions, but Aliy Zirkle, the first woman to win the Yukon Quest; Ray Redington, heir to the best known name in Iditarod mushing; and new veterans like Bruce Linton, who ran the race in 2006 and finished despite being diabetic and insulin dependent. Somewhere in the mix you had author (*Woodsong*) and musher Gary Paulsen, back for another try at the race, Native Alaskans Joe Garnie and Mike Williams, and many more.

Who you see and what stories you have to tell afterward are dependent on where you were at any given time. That's what makes it so special. Unlike other sporting events, there are no roped off areas, no restrictions on access to the athletes. It's a day made for stories and memories.

What kind of stories? A mish-mash of stories, some as simple as getting to coo over the latest Redington baby, another noting the reflection of Gov. Palin in a window behind Lance Mackey as he waited to draw a name for a prize drawing, and another as you wandered in search of specific mushers, usually finding someone else in the process. Retired mushers like Dan Seavey, whose roots go back to the original Iditarod, wandered about the crowd, as did perpetual fan favorite DeeDee Jonrowe.

Visually impaired Rachael Scdoris was there, ready for another run. She hoped recently injured Tim Osmar, who broke a leg in several places while protecting the Osmar homes from 2007 summer wildfires, would have recovered enough by race time to be her VI, or visual interpreter. Her VI's job is to help guide Rachel, who is classified as disabled due to her vision problems, along the trail.

Karen Ramstead holding a photo that shows her team,
including Snickers, the gray dog in lead, as she makes a presentation.

Amidst the crowd in 2007 was Canadian Karen Ramstead. She was there to sign up for the next race, yes, but she had a larger purpose in being there. The death of her main leader in last year's race, Snickers, had sent her searching for a way to bring meaning to the death of her beloved leader.

Ramstead had set up an account to help fund canine ulcer research in sled dogs. She was there to present the funds donated to date to vet/researcher Mike Davis. This was Ramstead's first picnic in person, so it will always hold special memories for her. That's a part of what makes the Iditarod so special, the memories, at once so personal and shared. From beginning to end, it's a unique experience for all involved.

Most mushers don't roll in until Friday, the day they'd be attending the annual Iditarod Official Finishers Club meeting, usually at Martin Buser's home, or even the next morning, although there are usually one or two mushers camped out in the parking lot in order to sign up near the top of the list of mushers. Those early birds are often drafted to help set up the tables and canopies that dot the yard.

The morning of the picnic, whether you arrive by chance or intent, it's usually clear that this is no normal day. The canopies unpacked by musher muscle the night before have been erected and now await guests, the volunteers that make the race happen. There is an even bigger indicator, however, that this isn't a normal day. There is usually no place to park. Most solve that little problem by parking along nearby roads or one year, the ditch along an adjoining road.

Throughout the day, one constant in recent years has been the arrival and departure of tour buses. Tourists pour from the buses, most seemingly unaware that they are in the midst of a hoard of mushers. I once watched one couple pose happily in front of the Iditarod's welcome sign. They were completely oblivious that the gentleman they'd politely shooed away for the photo was 5-time Iditarod Champion Rick Swenson. Is it any wonder the mushers, as well as most volunteers, now wear name-tags?

Of course, even with name tags, it's often difficult to put a name with the face of a musher. When we see them on the runners, whether live or on video, they somehow seem larger-than-life, so it's difficult to reconcile these average looking people with the image we so often carry in our minds. Surrounded by family and friends, dressed in "civvies," even the best known mushers tend to blend into the crowd. As a result, it brings home an element of fandom that is often missing, an element of appreciation for these athletes as people, not just images we encounter.

At first, fans, and that is truly what the volunteers are, tend to be shy. You'll see them huddle in small groups, pointing, trying to decide, "Is that Ray Jr.?" or "Where's Jeff? I just saw him!"

As for the mushers, while it would probably be erroneous to say they're all there because they enjoy the event, they do appreciate the volunteers' hard work. They make every effort to be available to fans despite the cloak of invisibility the lack of a parka and bib number offers them. They expect to be approached for photos and autographs and, in fact, most picnic veterans have learned to come prepared with their own supply of Sharpie pens. Some hand out musher cards or even mini- posters or booties, although those supplies dwindle quickly as the word spreads: "Joe Musher has posters!"

Through it all, a good time is had by all. Even though they know they're on display, the mushers enjoy the chance to hang out with fellow mushers without the competitive fires burning as much as the volunteers enjoy mingling with the mushers.

No matter where you stop or what direction you look, there's a new story or adventure awaiting you. By the time the announcement is made that "The food's ready!" dozens and dozens of stories have been shared, autographs secured and photos snapped. Most in attendance may be volunteers, but don't be mistaken, it's still a fan gathering. By this point in time, the rush of fandom has faded somewhat and it's become what it is advertised as being, a picnic. Names are being called over the loudspeaker to come and claim door prizes. Each volunteer was given a ticket as they signed in, so the action is non-stop.

The picnic meal was originally a pot-luck affair, each attendee bringing a dish. In recent years, this task has been taken on by caterers, however. Everyone, the volunteers and

Gary Paulsen signs a tee-shirt.

mushers alike, stands in line, tickets in hand, getting yet another opportunity to rub shoulders and get autographs from mushers whose names are known to most only via the media. Plates in hand, some picnic attendees stand to eat while chatting. Others find a spot on the lawn to spread out and eat, usually with friends or new friends they've just met. Even while this goes on, tour buses come and go and shoppers enter and leave the gift shop. It's a surreal experience, one in which you temporarily find yourself a part of the Iditarod show.

While most are eating, Iditarod officials and key volunteers — yes, even at their own picnic some work — are busy making final preparations for the musher sign-up process. As mushers arrive at Iditarod Headquarters, they are asked to sign in. The order of sign-in determines the order in which they will sign-up and draw their bib numbers for the next race.

In 2006, things were slightly different. That year the mushers on hand to sign-up got to pick any bib number still available when their turn came at the banquet. Determined to claim bib #13, Lance Mackey camped out for a week and was the first to sign up, going on to win the race. Mackey's father, Dick, and brother, Rick, both won the race wearing bib #13 on their sixth attempt.

Although the rules have changed this year, the sign-up process remains the same. After exchanging a few pleasantries with race officials, mushers turn in their paperwork and move on, leaving their spot to the next musher. As they exit, many are stopped by reporters for comments and, of course, asked for autographs. Savvy fans have figured out that this is the place to be at the picnic if you want to capture a photo and/or autograph from all those signing up.

It's a process that will continue for several hours. By 4 PM, many non-working volunteers will have drifted away clutching treasured autographs and a host of memories. Most mushers will remain, however.

Why?

By design, the Iditarod Trail Committee has traditionally tried to ensure their presence for the entire time by offering a few potential perks. Not only do those in attendance help determine when they'll pick their bib number, but those remaining until the very end are eligible for some tempting prizes, such as the refund of their entry fee, $3,000 in 2007. Needless to say, most mushers stick around for the drawings.

In many ways, the picnic is a return to the Iditarod spirit of old. Despite the pressures of competition, mushers fully realize that this race would not survive without its many volunteers. The volunteers are truly the heart of the Iditarod.

Some volunteers have well known faces, such as Susan Butcher, right, who helped check in John Baker, left, one year in Ruby as Al Marple watched.
Photo: Brenda Borden, www.duesouthphoto.com

Chapter 4

Volunteers:
The Heart of the Iditarod

Why volunteer?

For Eric Rogers, it was simple.

"I wanted to be part of Iditarod. I wanted to be part of something bigger than myself. Iditarod is made up of an incredible group of people, people who keep alive the dream of traveling across Alaska by dog team. I love walking into a room of Iditarod people and being part of the group. For me, it's about being owned by a shared passion."

Rogers' story is a bit different than that of other fans, however. While it started similarly, discovering the race and a passion for the dogs, it included a move to Alaska and discovering the shared camaraderie of the event. Rogers took it even one step further. He has run and finished the Iditarod.

Volunteers aren't just Alaskans, either. They come from all over the world. Linda Birchall came all the way from Atlanta, Georgia.

"I got involved because I loved the sheer adventure of a race across Alaska by men and women with dogs. I wanted to be 'on the inside,' to get a better feeling for why people race and to gain an understanding about it."

For most volunteers, learning about the race usually begins with a meeting held in January of that race year in either Anchorage or Wasilla. There, race officials run through the array of positions available, touting the pluses and minuses of each.

As noted at the Wasilla volunteer meeting in 2006, it's important that volunteers know exactly what they're getting themselves into. Many of the positions available are physically and even mentally demanding. Little sleep and lots of hard work, often in frigid temperatures, is part of a normal assignment.

For many positions, harsh as it sounds, the physically unfit need not apply. Don't fret, however, if you're not ready to run a race yourself. There are many positions and probably one that will suit your situation just fine, such as the Zuma email and phone room positions.

Positions not requiring lots of physical activity can often require long hours and dedication, however. Many volunteers start out at Race Headquarters, which is at the Millennium Alaskan Hotel in Anchorage. Positions there range from something as simple as being an errand runner to helping care for the dropped dogs, merchandise sales, answering phones or emails, or inputting information received from the trail into computers.

Anchorage's Rosemary Dunn is a Computer Room volunteer. "I like it because the Millennium Hotel is a short drive from home for me and it's the heart of the action. Every official piece of info from the trail gets funneled through there as does almost every other function (phone room, media, communications, etc.) is dependent on the accurate info getting out. Hitting the enter key to publish the info to the internet is kind of like pushing the throttle forward to take off in an airplane." A pilot, her comparison to the feeling of being part of it all, having not just an important role to play, but one that must be done accurately, is one most volunteers share.

"The flip side, of course, is entering the scratches," she notes. "That's real emotional for me. Even though we don't input the info until it's in our hands, with a form signed by race officials, publishing the info for all- the-world to see means you're making public the end of someone's dream . . . sometimes for a year, sometimes forever. It's not uncommon for me to cry when I have to do it."

Dropped dog area, Millennium Hotel

For many, the chance to work with the dogs is the pull. The Millennium is the dog drop location for much of the race and race volunteers often find a spot there. There's always a need for someone to scoop and idle observers have been known to find themselves sent off with a bucket to fetch water or perhaps find a needed item.

"I started out doing restart security," remembers Peg Moore, of Missouri. Grinning, knowing this writer was working as a rookie volunteer right beside her that year, she continues, "Remember us out there with the shovels?" Our job was not just to keep the crowd safely behind the fencing, but to shovel and rake the snow back into the middle of the chute area as it was kicked out by sled runners.

Moore, a vet tech, now works with dropped dogs. "I work with the two vets at the tough checkpoint of Millennium," she laughs. Most would agree. Dog drop there is a far cry from that on the trail or even in Nome, where workers often huddle in an unheated trailer car located on the outskirts of the dog lot.

"I love interacting with those wonderful dogs," declares Moore, "and working with veterinarians Jim Brick and Kobi Johnson is a blast."

I'll conclude with a memory from volunteer, now veteran Iditarod musher, Eric Rogers. It was one that took place when he was a trail volunteer. Trail positions are some of the most coveted volunteer assignments available.

"My favorite volunteer spot is working the trail," he declares, "particularly in a small, tight checkpoint. In Koyuk and Safety, accommodations were so limited one year that I was the only comms (communications) guy."

"I slept with my ham radio earphone in my ear," he remembers. Although he certainly can't explain how, he would recognize his call sign and wake up to converse with the person on the other end.

"The gentleman that opened the bar for us at Safety said he thought I was peculiar," laughs Rogers, "because in the middle of the night I'd sit up in bed and talk to myself."

Yep, the Iditarod can do that to you. Have you talking to yourself and planning your next trip back.

Chapter 5

Race Marshal: More Than a Job

Long time friends, Gary Paulsen and Mark Nordman.

"It's more than a job," says Iditarod Race Marshal Mark Nordman. "I want each and every musher that starts the race to get to Nome."

Nordman, who came to Alaska in 1976, first became interested in sled dog racing in Minnesota. He stumbled across a race in Duluth and then, the next year, was back as a volunteer. His job was far simpler than his current one. It was simply to watch the organizers public address system. That involved sleeping outside, however, to better watch over the equipment.

"I'd bought a brand new sleeping bag," Nordman laughs, "and was sleeping on a picnic table near an old, long-retired mail truck. The next morning, its back door rolled up and Tim White, who was sleeping inside with ten dogs, emerged. That was the beginning of my career in mushing."

It was also the beginning of a long relationship. As it turned out, White, one of the sport's best known names, had signed up to run the Knik 200 in Alaska the next year and needed a handler. Nordman made the journey with him, crossing the Northwest Territories and rolling into Alaska for the first time. He was 23 years old.

Asked to characterize White, Nordman pauses to think. "Sled dog sports are his life," he begins slowly. He explains that as being someone whose every thought and action is somehow connected to the dogs. "Tim White is the 'ultimate dog man'," concludes Nordman.

It should be noted here that although best known today in mushing circles as a race marshal, Nordman has had his share of success on the runners. He's run the Iditarod several times, but he's also run races in such diverse places as Canada and Argentina, using his own dogs, as well as Alaska and Minnesota. He won Montana's Race to the Sky in 1987. He's also had to scratch from the Iditarod (1994), giving him the benefit of understanding both ends of the racing spectrum.

"I've always loved the winter," he says, explaining his early fascination with the sport of sled dog racing. The John Beargrease, which originated in 1984, the year after Nordman's first Iditarod run and became one of the best known sled dog races in the world, drew Nordman. "I was involved there from Day One," he noted, "and even helped put the trail in." Mushing has always been a popular sport in Minnesota, he notes, drawing such legends as Alaska's

George Attla there in the late '70s to compete against Minnesota's best.

"I've been there," Nordman states firmly when asked his strength as a Race Marshal. He knows what it takes to get one team to Nome and that knowledge helps him in all his tasks as Race Marshal. Just as winning the Race to the Sky gave him a taste of what it means to win, having to scratch from the Iditarod taught him what it means for an entire year's work to come to nothing.

"I think I did well my first year as an Iditarod judge," he ponders, trying to explain what the Iditarod Trail Committee saw in him that led them to tap him as Race Marshal. He became Race Marshal the very next year. "I've always been one to critique myself. Being a dog musher, I know what they go through and that's important on the trail." He's comfortable with all aspects of the race ranging from what the mushers should have in their drop bags to what the dogs should look like on the trail, or what the musher should be doing to make progress down the trail.

"I love the race," he finally says simply. "I want every musher to finish. It's an emotional roller coaster, however. You have to figure out, as Paul Fleming (a past Race Marshal for many of the premiere Mid-West sled dog races) told me, 'Who owns the problem?' If we screwed up, we have to make it right. If the problem is, say, the result of bad training or the wrong food or supplies being sent out by the musher, however, that's your problem as a musher."

How deeply ingrained is the Iditarod in his life?

"It used to be that I couldn't do anything, go anywhere, without looking at it through the eyes of how it worked for the dogs." In other words, he'd walk into a hardware store, see a snap or cable on display and immediately think of how he could use it for the dogs. Hmm, reminds me of his own description of another dog man, Tim White. Now, while he says the Iditarod is a part of him, he isn't quite that bad. He does have a team but although he admits to some occasional thoughts of returning to competition, he notes it's most helpful right now in helping him stay on top of the various advances in care and equipment.

As a result, when Nordman stands up in front of the rookies assembled at the mandatory rookie meeting in December, he knows just what they're thinking. He also knows what they need to know. The rookie meeting, once a brief, one day session, has expanded under his guidance and now takes several days.

"It used to be in the meeting room at Iditarod Headquarters," he recalls, "on the Wednesday before the race."

Why did it change?

"You can't teach much at that point. By that time, too many things have to be in place, such as your drop bags. All of your planning and training is complete. You can't expect a musher to make many real changes that late in the game. Nowadays, if a rookie takes good notes, by the time they leave the meetings, they can save themselves money because they know what to buy and not buy."

Four-time champion Martin Buser hosts a hands-on session at his kennel, for instance, as part of the planned information sharing. This gives rookies an opportunity to see how one of the most successful mushers ever does things. It also gives race officials a chance to get to know the rookies in a bit less formal atmosphere. It helps, as Nordman observes, to know the inter-relationships between mushers, too.

One thing rookies will find that has changed little over the years is the list of mandatory gear items. It's a pretty stable list, says Nordman, adding that Joe May has often said a shovel would make more sense than snowshoes at times, however. Clothing and gear is high tech and light weight, but remains the same in name as it did back when the race began.

If Nordman could magically change one thing about qualifying for the race, he'd like to see a better job being done by mushers and officials to prepare them to race. His goal isn't to keep anyone out, instead it's to keep them in, but make it a better experience for both musher and dogs. Things have changed so drastically in dog care since the early days of the race that the musher must now be a virtual fountain of knowledge on a variety of topics, ranging from high tech gear to animal husbandry and nutrition to proper gear selections, genetics of dogs, even human and animal muscle tone and development.

Nordman works just as hard to make sure smaller races are successful as he does to help the individual mushers. He's been to Europe and South America and while in South America even competed with his own dogs. It is actions such as these that have resulted in the popularity of the sport growing internationally. Such actions are instrumental in spreading the importance of better and better dog care around the world. Thus, while we might visualize Nordman hard at work only during race time, his job description as Iditarod Race Marshal is only the tip of the iceberg.

Oddly enough, when asked to define the term Race Marshal, Nordman went the other way. He wants to avoid being seen as a traffic cop, so to speak, as he knows some view him. An affable, friendly man, he tries to make sure he is in a race hub, such as McGrath, every night of the race for better communication overall.

In addition to being chairman of the Rules Committee, he's also 'Village Relations Coordinator.' This is a job he enjoys and takes seriously. He tries to spend time outside of the race with village elders and leaders, who, in his opinion, are often the forgotten cogs that make the race a success. They don't ask for a great deal, he notes, but they do like to have their efforts recognized.

"Without their involvement," he firmly declares, "we wouldn't have an Iditarod." Jeff Shultz, the Iditarod's official photographer, helps with this effort, providing what Nordman dubbed 'appreciation photos' or posters for the villages after each race.

Speaking of being recognized, it's was a running joke among the long-time Iditarod loyal that Nordman and former Race Manager Jack Niggemyer were considered almost interchangeable.

Not true, laughs Nordman, although they worked together well. Niggemyer retired prior to Iditarod 2006.

Asked to distinguish the jobs in simple terms, something that proves elusively difficult to do, Nordman notes that the Race Manager is primarily involved in pre-race logistics, the things that make the race happen, the things that will get the dog teams up the trail to Nome. Nordman, on the other hand, as Race Marshal, is involved with the competitive aspects of the race itself and in constant, often intense interaction with the mushers. That's where his experience as a musher himself comes into play. Yet, while accepting that as Race Marshal he is the one who bears the final responsibility for decisions, he emphasizes that he depends heavily upon his eight judges. The Iditarod, no matter on what level, is about teamwork.

While most see Nordman as calm, a laid back personality, someone who rarely loses his cool, he admits he gets emotionally involved.

"I worry," he admits. "I take it to heart."

For Nordman, it's more than a job, especially when he has to deal with mushers after one of the worst things that can happen to a musher has happened, the death of a dog.

Kjetil Backen's loss of Tok in 2004, for instance, took place at the worst possible time. Backen was just about to enter Unalakleet. He was the first musher to arrive. That musher is presented with an award. Nordman, however, was notified just before Backen's arrival, asking him to meet Backen just outside of the checkpoint. He knew immediately that there was a problem.

Distraught, with an expired dog that had given no signs of problems prior to collapsing; Backen was ready to scratch from the race. Fully understanding the depth of Backen's despair, it was up to Nordman to counsel him and urge the best action. Even now, Nordman's eyes get a faraway look in them as he remembers that moment, the pain he felt for Backen and how difficult a decision it was for both of them. Backen would finish. After the death of her beloved leader Snickers in 2007, Karen Ramstead, who would scratch, had only praise for Nordman's kindness and assistance during that difficult time.

"It's more than a job," Nordman declares again firmly.

Nordman's scariest memory, at least one of them, involved a musher, however, not a dog. He was in Anvik in 1989 when he got a call saying musher Mike Madden had been found lying alongside the trail. He'd been found by fellow musher Jamie Nelson, who was soon joined by a group of mushers that included Mitch Brazin, Linwood Fiedler, Kathy Halverson and Jerry Austin. Madden was sick and delirious. While Austin and Fiedler, judged to have the fastest teams available, mushed ahead to Iditarod, the closest checkpoint, to recruit help, the others stayed behind with Madden, administering fluids and trying to keep him comfortable and warm.

Then Race Manager Jack Niggemyer was able to get a National Guard helicopter out to where they were camped. While Austin mushed Madden's team into the Iditarod checkpoint, the helicopter flew Madden to the hospital in Anchorage. According to the doctors, had another two hours passed, Madden would have most likely died.

Nordman also remembers the frantic search for musher Bob Ernisse, now deceased, who had become lost in one of the infamous coastal storms. Another fearful moment was when the plane of one of the race veterinarians, Dr. Jim Leech, crashed at Cripple. Many of these moments are invisible to fans, but to Nordman and other race officials, there are truly moments like this that make their job a matter of life and death.

How has the race changed since his early days with it as a musher?

"We came up with a fully over-loaded half ton truck," he remembers fondly of his first trip to Alaska with Tim White. "We had about a dozen dogs, four thread-bare tires and we had to drive slowly the entire way. It was a grand trip. Now, for some new mushers, not all, however, they'll get here and you ask 'em how their trip went and they'll say, 'Oh, man, it was awful. The CD player broke before we even got halfway.'" The mind-set has changed.

So, too, has the experience.

"In my first race, I got lost the first night and was passed by a lot of teams. That was the beginning, but what a fun trip it was," he remembers. "Now, mushers can go for miles and miles and miles and not even see another musher."

How would Nordman characterize today's mushers, especially those who have been most successful? Why are some able to be successful and keep being successful year after year?

"They're driven," he explains. "It wouldn't matter what they set their minds to, they'd be a success at whatever they set out to do."

"The Iditarod is the Super Bowl, Kentucky Derby, World Cup and Tour de France all rolled together," Nordman says, completely understanding the draw of the race. Everyone works together and knows the others' strengths and weaknesses. That's what makes it so successful. The Iditarod is, after all, about teamwork.

Chapter 6

The Rookie Meeting:
Mentoring the Iditarod's Future

Martin Buser talks to 2007 Iditarod rookies at his Happy Trails Kennel.

"You have control over one team and only one dog team," Martin Buser told the 2007 Iditarod rookies gathered in his living room. They were there as part of the annual rookie meeting.

"Don't pay attention to other teams. Don't mimic others. Do what's right for your team."

Pens and pencils flashed as rookies rushed to write down every bit of trail-proven wisdom flowing from Buser's mouth. After all, it isn't every day a rookie musher gets to sit down and ask questions of a four-time Iditarod champion.

2006 was Martin Buser's fourth year of hosting the group. Although they had spent the day before in similar meetings in Anchorage, for many rookies this was their first visit to an Iditarod champion's kennel.

Rookies are always an interesting mix and the wide-eyed wonder of some was obvious. Others, such as Copper Basin winner Allen Moore, came with a wealth of knowledge about mushing, but as a rookie in the 2007 Iditarod, understood that this was a whole different race. Winning a mid-distance race does not automatically translate to easily becoming a successful Iditarod musher and Moore understood this. "I've got lots of questions," he noted, biding his time to ask them.

"I wish they'd done this when I was a rookie," mused Buser about the rookie meetings. He encouraged the rookies to ask questions, questions he knew that he, as a four-time Iditarod winner, might forget to answer.

While they were initially slow in coming, once the first few questions came forth, others came more quickly and easily.

"Finishing in Nome puts you in an elite group of athletes," Buser told the group. To date, only 637 people have completed the Iditarod. The process of becoming an Iditarod Finisher is something that those who've never run the race cannot understand, Buser noted, perhaps as much by way of cautioning them as advising them. "You'll be changed forever."

Buser emphasized that the ability to get past the lows of the race is where the stories come from. It's also what gets you to Nome.

"You *will* feel like quitting," he told them. "When you do, go to sleep."

Expanding on that, Buser added that fatigue and frustration can get in the way of making sound decisions. "Shut down and rest. Find a corner and go to sleep. Do not scratch." In fact, he told them to put his name on a list of three people that they pledged to call before they made any final decision to scratch.

"It gives reflection time," he explained, going on to note that so many aspects of this race are mind over matter. "I won't be returning calls," he added with a grin, leaving them to figure that one out on their own.

Of course, while mind over matter may be a vital aspect of finishing the Iditarod, there are 1,049 miles that must be traveled between Anchorage and the Burled Arch in Nome. Buser's advice was very down to earth and practical here, with the emphasis on being prepared, consistent, and getting into routines now during training that would help shape a successful run to Nome.

Watching Buser demonstrate with a family pet how he puts on booties, one of the things that immediately became apparent was the lack of wasted effort. The movement was swift and sure, the task completed almost in the blink of an eye. Left front, right front, turn, then repeat with the dogs' rear legs. Everything is practiced and fine-tuned, booties placed in the same pockets during training runs as for the race, and packaged together for ease of access. Checkpoint routines must be the same, he noted, emphasizing the importance of nutrition, sleep and hydration for the musher, too.

"Set rules and follow them during training," a handout instructed. "Become like a robot. Don't wait for the race to implement." In other words, get into the routine now, not on 4th Avenue.

It's the same with Buser's Happy Trails kennel outside. Routine is the key. Color-coded harnesses wait on a centrally located stand, while dog houses are arranged to allow for efficiency of movement during feeding and clean-up. Kennel runs are interconnected, saving steps. The Buser dogs are eating the same food they'll be eating in March, I might note, something emphasized by Buser.

"You need to fuel them properly right now," he declared. That's what it's all about: Doing the right thing now so that success will come in Nome.

Chapter 7

Iditarod Veterinarians
Lend a Hand

Stu Nelson, 2003

"People need to understand that if an animal isn't well cared for, it can't perform, so good care, not neglect, is the norm."

"Mushers are usually the first to see any sort of abnormality," continues the Iditarod's chief vet, Stu Nelson. He's quick to point out that the veterinarians and mushers work together. "The vets have been educated and know what to look for on the trail, often seeing things even before the team stops. The mushers are on the front line, however. They know their dogs better than anyone. They keep records in a vet diary throughout the race and have it available for the vets and signed at every checkpoint."

Aliy Zirkle, right, waits as her vet book is checked at Ruby.
Photo: Brenda Borden, www.duesouthphoto.com

How do they do it?

Nelson reminded me that the dogs have already gone through extensive pre-race exams. He gave me an acronym to explain the basic steps taken: **HAWL.**

H stands for heart and hydration, something of the utmost importance to both musher and vet. The vets specifically check for elevated heart rates (greater than 120 bpm at rest) and abnormal rhythms (arrhythmias). It has been noted that most sled dogs have a heart rate of less than 100 beats per minute. That's fit, very fit, as house dogs normally have a heart rate of about 120. In any case, the heart aspect of this acronym is obvious, but mushers also do what might be called the "snap back" test to check a dog's hydration. Basically, they pull the skin between the dogs' shoulders up and watch to see if it "snaps" back into place quickly. The speed with which the skin resumes its normal appearance is a good indication of the dog's hydration level.

A stands for both appetite and attitude, important ingredients for success. What the vet is looking for here is to see that the dog is not only eating but having a positive race. As simplistic as it sounds, good attitude makes for a happy, healthy dog, so, according to Nelson, it's high on the list of things to check.

W stands for weight, which might be seen as a logical partner of "hydration" and "appetite." If an animal is eating well and has a good appetite, but has difficulty keeping on weight, it's going to be losing strength as the race progresses. This would mean more time and attention will have to be paid it by the musher during both runs and rests. These dogs might even have to be coaxed to eat or drink, meaning more care must be given.

Finally, **L** is for "lungs." Is the dog having trouble breathing? Are there any obvious obstructions in the air passages? Are there any signs of impending disease or problems? Again, this brief explanation makes this sound simplistic, but the techniques used have been effective, according to Nelson. The most common reason for dropping a dog is some sort of limp, a visual sign, so a method of determining other, less visible indications of a potential problem, is a valuable tool.

I've observed the veterinarian crew at the dropped dog area in Anchorage several times. At first the procedure might seem random. Look closely, however, and you'll note they are going thru the exact same procedure time after time. If you stop long enough to listen and watch, you'll note that every dog is treated as an individual. They're greeted by name, easily available on the report that is returned from the checkpoint where they've been dropped. Ears and bellies are scratched and rubbed while the dogs are reminded what

"Good dogs!" they are. Only then does the actual exam begin.

A volunteer vet checks a dog at Ruby.
Photo: Brenda Borden, www.duesouthphoto.com

Hands gently probe all joints and body areas, limbs are stretched and flexed, and temperatures are taken; all the steps described above in the explanation of the HAWL method. Despite being surrounded by strangers, often not just the vets and volunteers, but fans who've walked out from the hotel to observe, most dogs take the exam in stride. Volunteers are constantly refreshing the straw supply and busy cleaning up, proof that what goes in, must come out. The exam itself is often accompanied by the seemingly perpetual flash of cameras as fans approach to watch and snap photos. Questions are often asked and answered.

Perhaps one of the more impressive moments I've seen is that the routine didn't vary from this relaxed, methodical procedure even when the wind chill dipped to fifty below outside one year. Dogs were gently unloaded from planes and crates and acknowledged as individuals, each called by name, and only then, despite the harsh temperatures and winds, did exams begin. Dog coats were nearby, ready to be put on dogs needing them and straw, always abundant, simply became more so, allowing dogs to curl up in the warmth it so naturally provides. Those needing any further attention were taken to local clinics nearby.

While Nelson acknowledges the ultimate goal, no dog deaths during the race, hasn't been met, he knows statistics back him up. I asked him for an example. His answer was that the risk to Iditarod dogs fell somewhere between that to a human jogger and cross country skier.

To put this in perspective without getting into actual statistics, if 84 teams leave the starting line, there will be 1,344 dogs on the trail. The race lasts two weeks, often longer depending upon the weather and speed of the back of the pack. The likelihood of each and every dog remaining safe and sound is unlikely, much as we'd like it to be different.

Of course, there are also lighter moments on the trail. In this day and age, race officials tend to know where each musher is located and when one is expected into the next checkpoint. When volunteers and officials are told it'll be such and such time when the next team comes in, most take advantage of the break to catch some sleep. This was the case one year in Koyuk, which is where mushers go out over the sea ice. Volunteers had been busy but it appeared there should be at least a two hour gap before the next team came in. Most settled in for a power nap.

"Musher coming in!!!"

It was 2 a.m. and no one should have been coming in. Surprised volunteers and vets scrambled for boots and parkas and rushed out to meet the incoming team. The problem was, it was just a team. No musher. He'd fallen off. The dogs had left him far, far behind. Rather than stop, the dogs had simply continued, little caring whether the musher was with them or not. In fact, laughed Nelson, the team had even parked itself.

The surprised checkpoint group eventually reunited musher and dogs but one can only imagine the ribbing that musher took, and most likely still takes when they pull into Koyuk.

Okay, other than the ability to park itself, what sort of dog do mushers and vets see as the ideal racing sled dog?

"The ideal sled dog today isn't the stereotypical sled dog of the past," Nelson notes. "It will weigh about fifty pounds and can be of any breed." That, of course, is as long as it meets ISDMA standards and can be classified as a Northern Breed. "It obviously has to pass some pretty rigorous exams to qualify, but must also display the willingness and desire to pull a sled."

Nelson cautioned, just because a dog meets these criteria didn't necessarily mean it will be a sled dog. It has to want to run. "It has to have the proper training and conditioning, too," he notes, "to adequately prepare it for racing."

In other words, just because I have an Alaskan husky sleeping on my couch and shedding on my rug, that doesn't mean I can take her out and hook her to a sled and get to Nome, even with a prior finish under her dog collar. Without the proper specialized care, training, and conditioning, even the best sled dogs cannot perform.

Chapter 8

Organized Chaos:
Drop Bags

    One of the biggest pre-race chores faced by mushers is that of organizing their drop bags. For those outside of Alaska, getting the bags to Alaska is quite an undertaking itself.

    "Having done it three times," remembers musher spouse Maureen Morgan, "I can guarantee it takes a lot of time, planning and organization. What goes in what bag and where is important."

The drop bags are provided to each musher by the Iditarod Trail Committee. Each bag will eventually contain an average of 60 pounds of gear and/or food per checkpoint. Bags needing to remain frozen will have the word "Freeze" stenciled on them. Some mushers indicate how many bags they're sending to each checkpoint on each, too, perhaps 1 of 3 or 3/3, ensuring they'll know how many to look for at each checkpoint. Most mushers also carry a list with them of what they have waiting.

The first task is to pack the bags. Organization and room to spread out are essential. While methods vary, most mushers spread out the bags according to checkpoint. The items to be packed for that particular checkpoint are placed beside its bags. One indication of how long a musher plans to stay at any given checkpoint is quantity. The more supplies packed, the longer they plan to stay at that checkpoint.

All those bags don't pack themselves. "Imagine your living room or driveway completely covered by large bags," says Maureen Morgan. "Every spot is covered, if not with bags, with the items to go into them."

Ed and Tasha Stielstra can sympathize. They used their living room for part of the project.

"The entire house was pretty much a disaster for three days," sighs Tasha, an accomplished, winning musher herself. "Booties, runner plastic, socks, pants, underwear, batteries, tissues, dog jackets, foot ointment and harnesses were spread out everywhere!" This is definitely one aspect of race preparation most fans can't even begin to imagine. Brenda Borden, wife of Iditarod 2002 musher Bill Borden, remembers how the smell of the meat and fish they packed remained in their garage long after the race.

Morgan remembers spending days in the kitchen just preparing her husband Bob's food bags. "Each item was cooked, frozen and then put into a food saver, airtight bag," she says. On the trail the musher will "take these bags and drop them into the cooker as they are melting snow for water for the dogs. Yes, they share the same cooker," she chuckles.

Karen Ramstead's 2007 drop bags wait in the dog lot to be loaded for delivery to a central point. Photo: Donna Quante

Of course, mushers must eat, too. While different mushers have different menus, the preparation of the people food is just as important as that of the dog food. If the mushers aren't properly fueled, they can't care for their dogs. Ed Stielstra's menu included beef stew, spaghetti, tuna casserole, halibut, shrimp pasta, lasagna, pumpkin pie, cheesecake and cookies. All were vacuum sealed to retain their freshness and take up less room.

Once packed, the bags are shipped to Alaska by those living outside the state or carried up when mushers drive up with the dogs. The Stielstras, who live in Michigan, were able to use a giant grocery freezer to freeze the meat extra hard. Bags were then packed, checked and sealed for repackaging into three 48" x 40" x 6' insulated boxes and put on a truck headed to Seattle. From there, they were taken by barge to Anchorage, Alaska.

Of course, it isn't just mushers from the Lower 48 that ship their bags to Anchorage rather than deliver them in person. I've spied bags with names like those of two Alaskan mushers, Redington and Seavey being unloaded at the drop bag facility from semi-trucks. Let's take a look at how the bags are handled when they're delivered by the mushers themselves.

For mushers in the Anchorage area, the procedure starts with a drive to the shipping point, where loaded dog trucks are backed up to the shipping door. From there, volunteers will unload the bags and begin the process of sorting them into piles to be flown to the checkpoints later. While some volunteers are unloading these trucks, others are unloading semi-trucks arriving at the facility doors with bags from all over.

For all those involved, it's quite important to keep your wits about you. Everything is happening at the same time and for multiple mushers concurrently. As a result, although I'm presenting the next few steps as a series of events, they're ongoing and happen over and over and over again until the last bag is in place. Later they'll be loaded onto a plane to be flown to the proper checkpoint by the Iditarod Air Force.

Volunteers collect and move drop bags, 2007.
Photo: Donna Quante, www.huskyproductions.net

Volunteers move the bags toward a table at the front of the storage facility. This is usually done in something of an assembly line fashion to relieve the burden. When the bags reach a table set up along one wall, they're placed on a scale built into the floor to be weighed. A volunteer calls out the weight, which is then recorded by those seated at adjacent tables. Of course, the weighing is of great interest to the mushers as that determines how big a check they'll be leaving behind at the end of the day to pay the shipping costs to send the bags to the various checkpoints.

The bags are then passed along to be piled onto a stack of bags designated for that checkpoint. Different colors on the bags and different colored lettering is designed to make the bags easier to sort. Standing name posts mark the site for each checkpoint's bags. Interesting enough, there's usually an empty pallet for Safety. Since few mushers stay there long, few send bags to Safety, the last checkpoint before Nome.

Piles of drop bags sorted for different checkpoints.
Photo: Donna Quante, www.huskyproductions.net

Throughout the day, this process is repeated and repeated. Finally, of course, the mushers must face the music and ante up the cost, while elsewhere, another truckload is being unloaded and the process continues.

Yes, it's hard work, but it is fun, too, and friendships are formed that last a lifetime.

So are traditions. Donna Quante, who went with Karen Ramstead to drop of her 2007 bags, reports, "When the checkers got a bag for Shaktoolik, they'd say the name loudly, then the weight, then the name again and all the people in line would go, 'Woo, woo, woo' in deep voices like a football game chant. It was funny and there were always giggles after it happened."

Volunteer Steve Walker, who was there working, perhaps says it best. "The Shak chant has been going on as long as I've been there." He paused and grinned. "I'll be going to Shak during the race. Maybe we should do the chant as each musher comes in."

"It's little things like that which keep spirits high and people willing to help," he continues. "It becomes a fun environment even though a lot of hard work gets done."

Chapter 9

EKGs, Meetings and Banquets,
Oh, My

One of Karen Ramstead's Siberian Huskies reaches out a
paw for reassurance during the EKG examination.

Did you ever wonder what the mushers are up to during
the week prior to the Iditarod? Sitting around relaxing,
right? No, the week prior to the start of the Iditarod is jam
packed for them. While taking care of their dogs and keeping
them loose and ready to go is a given, there are a multitude
of "must do" activities in which they are required to
participate.

One of those activities involves having blood work and
electrocardiograms, EKGs for short, done on their team
dogs. This is done in a variety of centrally located places

earlier in the month, but for those unable to get to one of these locations, this chore is crowded into the week before the race, too. For mushers, it's a time of unloading dogs and taking them in and out of the trailer.

Photo: Donna Quante, www.huskyproductions.net

Ironically, as they reach the trailer to be utilized that's temporarily parked in the parking lot of Iditarod Headquarters, one of the sites used, the dogs meet one of what they seem to consider the scariest obstacles in the entire Iditarod, climbing the grated steps into the trailer. As a result, you'll see most mushers carrying dog after dog up the steps and into the trailer.

Once inside, dogs are soothed by handlers and mushers as the vet tech team swings into action. The procedure involves a series of steps. Just inside the doorway, a handler or assistant will hold the dog for blood drawing. Most straddle the dog just as they would for putting on a harness or booties, although the dog's head is held high in this instance. This allows technicians to find a vein easier. The blood is drawn into a vial and labeled. It will then be put into a centrifuge machine which separates the compounds. Labels are also affixed to the record sheets of each dog, assuring the paperwork will match up to the dog in question.

This procedure usually involves two people, the technician and the handler. The next step may involve a few more. After the blood is drawn, the dog is moved to an examination table. There, it is laid on its side, not always an easy task, and a few moments are taken to soothe and comfort the confused dogs. Clips are sprayed to clear away any residual oils or fur from previous dogs and then attached to strategic points to check pulse rates. The clips don't hurt. I've even tried them on my own fingers.

As the musher or a designated person soothes the dog at its head, readings are taken by a portable monitor and printed out to be attached to the rest of the dog's health paperwork. If there are any questionable results, another evaluation is run immediately, just to be sure. This goes on all day, with musher after musher unloading and bringing in dog after dog to be tested.

This is in addition to a regular examination by a vet certified by the Iditarod Trail Committee, ensuring that the testing is done by those familiar with working sled dogs.

Other activities are also going on. At the mandatory meeting on the Thursday before the start, mushers receive the most up-to-date trail information available. While waiting for the information portion of the meeting to begin, all mushers are busy signing the cache envelopes they will carry up the trail to Nome as well as renewing old friendships and making new ones. Somewhere in the midst of all this, sponsors and race officials are introduced. Then the meeting room is cleared of all but mushers and race officials for the remainder of the meeting. Information is shared and questions are answered.

Later, mushers have lunch at the Millennium Alaskan Hotel with their Idita-Riders. This is an informal luncheon, one designed simply to allow musher and rider to meet prior to the start. Pizza seems to be the norm and although brief, the lunch ensures that no rider arrives at a dog truck on Saturday a total stranger to their musher.

Finally, Thursday evening, mushers will travel to the Sullivan Arena for the annual Musher Banquet. This is a public event, one where fans take advantage of their proximity to gather autographs and snag photos. In the past, mushers have drawn their numbers at the afternoon meeting or on stage at the banquet. In other words, they had no choice in starting position other than sheer luck and didn't know their draw until it was announced. In 2006, a new twist was added. Mushers were called to the stage in the order they'd signed up, the normal routine, but once on the stage were able to pick the desired starting number from those remaining.

In other words, the earlier you signed up, the more chance you had of getting a desired starting spot. Most simply picked the first and lowest available number for Iditarod 2006, although the eventual winner and an early sign-up, Jeff King, picked bib number 30. Doug Swingley, the eventual second place winner, picked bib 5, while third place winner Paul Gebhardt started at the very back, picking #84. The procedure went back to the numbers being drawn in 2008.

Most likely, somewhere in the midst of all these required appearances, between running and caring for their dogs, mushers will also be meeting with fans, friends and supporters, or perhaps even hosting an open house. I've attended breakfasts and dinners intended to thank both, some more formal than others, but all relaxed and upbeat. For example, Jeff King often spends an afternoon at the Aurora Art Gallery in downtown Alaska with his artist wife Donna Gates. There they meet and greet both race fans and art lovers. If you're lucky, there might even be a dog or two around. Other mushers are doing similar stints elsewhere, all designed to thank those who've helped make their dream possible. The Iditarod is a team effort, after all.

Chapter 10

Pre-Race Vet Checks

Depending on what your goals are, a visit to Iditarod Headquarters the Wednesday before the race might be viewed as a fan's dream or nightmare.

It will quickly be obvious this isn't a normal day at Headquarters. As you turn into the driveway, you're likely to be met by a line of dog trucks stretching back nearly as far as the arch over the driveway. If you come to shop, this may not be a good day, if only because you will probably wind up parked around the corner, then around another corner and down the road, or maybe even around the corner and down the road in an adjoining parking lot. Yes, it can be that crowded!

On the other hand, if you are there to see mushers and Iditarod dogs, this is a great day to be at Iditarod Headquarters. Mushers are required to have their dog team checked over one last time during the week prior to the race and, for most, this is the day. This is apart from the EKG and bloodwork testing done earlier. The veterinary team put together by Chief Iditarod Vet Stu Nelson is on hand, performing the checks at no cost to the mushers. Nelson himself can usually be seen amongst the vet crew, taking a hands-on approach to his role as Chief Vet.

The procedure seen here mirrors Nelson's **HAWL** acronym, discussed in Chapter Seven. Just to review:

H stands for heart and hydration, something of the utmost importance to both musher and vet. **A** stands for appetite and attitude, two more important ingredients for success. **W** stands for weight. **L** is for lungs.

Jr. Iditarod musher Jordan Lolley soothes Hazel, one of his father Bill Borden's team dogs in 2002. Hazel, AKA Hazy, now lives with the author.
Photo: Brenda Borden, www.duesouthphoto.com

Those gathered in the Iditarod's parking lot can watch vets go through this routine countless times. Every dog potentially slated to run the race must have this exam. Although some mushers do opt to have their own private veterinarians do the exams, that means somewhere in the vicinity of 2000 Iditarod dogs are having this same evaluation at about the same time.

Did I mention that it can be cold? I live six miles from Iditarod Headquarters and woke up to a balmy -3 degrees one vet check morning. A former Floridian, I sympathized with first time visitors who haven't yet discovered the wonder of hand and foot warmers. Camera batteries quickly froze, creating the necessity of changing batteries frequently, even for those of us who knew the trick of sticking a warmer in a pocket with spare batteries.

Despite this, a steady stream of observers made their way up and down the icy parking lot, many with camera, race program and pen in hand, hoping to get an early autograph. Sans bibs, of course, most mushers simply blend in with the rest of us, so it wasn't unusual for fans to dart up to those with some visible familiarity with the mushers and ask in a rush, "Who's that?" pointing toward the suspected musher. Some huddled inside, watching mushers being interviewed by the media, marveling at being a part of it all.

Through it all, dog trucks arrived and departed. Dogs were dropped and checked. Then, room was made for the next musher. It's just one more hurdle on the way to Iditarod 2006 for the mushers, but a great photo opportunity for fans.

Gary Paulsen gives his Idita-Rider a ride down Cordova Hill in Anchorage.
Photo: Jan DeNapoli, www.muzzyssplace.net

Chapter 11

Idita-Riders Do It on the Trail

2004 Idita-Rider patch. Photo: Betty Walden

"On by, on by!"

Quickly snapping to attention, Team Stormwatch's Slick Willie responded to his musher's voice. The only difference is that musher Wayne Curtis' voice was coming from the video playing in the living room of Willie's new owner Paulette Jones. Jones rode in Curtis' sled in 1997. Willie remembered his commands; he was just a tad bewildered as to what he was supposed to be going "on by."

"I started following Iditarod in 1988," remembers Jones. "1997 was the 25th anniversary of Iditarod as well as my 25th wedding anniversary, so we thought that might be a good anniversary trip." In order to become an Idita-rider, one must bid for and win one of the coveted spots.

Jones made a list of 5-6 mushers, then decided she really couldn't afford any of the big name ones (Martin, DeeDee, Jeff, etc). As a result, she chose Curtis' all-Siberian team. "I've owned Siberians since 1973," she noted.

I ask her what she remembers being told at the Idita-Rider meeting.

She laughs. "The only thing I remember is to 'keep your mouth closed,' I guess because the dogs might throw flying poop at you. I was so excited that I can't remember anything else they told me. It was way too short a ride. I would have loved to go another 50 miles."

"My best memory was gliding under the start banner. After all the years of seeing that in pictures, actually being there was the best," she declares.

"Then I heard *my* name over the loudspeaker: 'Paulette Jones from Maryland.' That was really cool. I never turned around to look at the musher (or tag sled driver), and I should have because that was fun, too. I was so hypnotized by those 12 dogs, that long line of dogs out front listening to Wayne's voice, that I just wanted to watch them work."

"Going around a corner, the sled was on one runner. Wayne was laughing, assuring me, 'I won't spill you, don't worry.' Then we got passed by another team, and all I could hear was the hiss of the runners." She smiled, remembering. "Oh, and the muffins. That's so awesome to have the muffins tossed at you. And people standing everywhere with the newspaper yelling 'Good luck, Wayne.' Tailgate parties, so to speak. Going over the walkways over a major highway, that was neat, under the roads, inside those pipes. Our team went right on through."

"It was just so cool. Nothing like it. When I watched my video of it, I could hear Wayne's voice shouting 'On by, on by.' I had adopted one of his retired sled dogs and that dog, Willie, would stare at the TV and listen to Wayne's voice, trying to decide, I guess, 'just WHAT am I supposed to be DOING right now?' It was hilarious."

Deep sigh. "Just thinking about it again makes me want to do it again. And I thought it was a once in a life time thing."

It's an enthusiasm others feel.

"Being from Texas I never see snow, much less have a chance to ride in a sled," said Betty Walden. "There's still a bit of a kid in me and I just had to do it!"

"What a thrill it was to wave back to the crowd and feel the cold wind in my face," she remembers.

Although she hasn't done the Idita-Rider program a second time, she has gone one step further. Her musher, GB Jones, who wasn't running in 2006, invited her out to his kennel where he has a short course set up to allow fans and friends to experience driving a team themselves.

"I made two loops before falling down gracefully," she laughs. "What a thrill. I'd waited 76 years for this Idita-Ride and then got to play musher."

Carole Parsons "loved being down in the trenches with the mushers," she says. She rode with Nelson Shughart in 2000. It cost the equivalent of a month's salary, she notes. Although she has returned to the Iditarod, she has done so as a handler, a common route for Idita-Riders physically capable of taking on this task.

Teacher Kathy Kent was an Idita-rider in 2003 with Frank Sihler. It was his rookie year. She video-taped the ride and an interview with Sihler as part of a DVD now used every year in school.

"I first heard about the program when I saw a report on the TV news about a celebrity having a ride and then saw the information on Iditarod.com," she recalls.

Besides the obvious, she remembers the extraction part at the end of the trip. This is where the Idita-Rider's experience ends with the musher and they have time to focus on other things, such as other Idita-Riders.

"It was nice to meet the other riders since you were familiar with them in code during the bidding process," says Kathy. "One person would introduce himself and add his code name. We would sigh or comment remembering this person getting his bid and bidding you out."

Claudia Nowak, Ed Stielstra's Idita-Rider for many years, remembers the kindness of the Stielstra's.

"Ed Stielstra, his family, and handlers were exceedingly nice to me. They know that I have MS and they always had a spot for me to sit down while waiting. They always bring a grill and have hot food and snacks galore."

"There are always lots of hands helping me when I'm walking around and getting in and out of the sled. Volunteers (called ejectors) are waiting to help you out of the sled. There is always a warm place to wait for the bus and hot soup, cookies, and hot chocolate are provided," she adds.

For anyone fearing certain health issues might hinder your participation, read on.

"Deby Trosper (the program coordinator) has been wonderful to us," continued Nowak. "She knows that I have a visual impairment and my balance is not good. She arranged for a snowmachine to give me a ride from the Cabela's bus down to the staging area where the dog trucks were. I also rode the snowmachine back up the hill to the bus." There was a blind teacher who rode in a sled in 2006.

Nowak and her husband Lee have both been Idita-Riders.

"It makes us feel a part of the race."

The Nowaks live in Michigan and try to support Michigan mushers such as Stielstra whenever possible. "We have volunteered at almost 30 sled dog races in the past 6 winters here in Michigan. We personally know all these guys. We have visited their kennels, gone out on training runs, and held their sleds in the chutes. We take pictures of them at races and mail the pictures to them. We are big supporters of sled dog races in Michigan, hence our choice of Michigan mushers."

Ed Stielstra leads his team to the start line with
Claudia Nowak in the sled as Idita-Rider.

"Everything about being an Idita-Rider is great fun. We were issued VIP passes which allowed us to go in restricted areas at the ceremonial start and the restart. We really liked walking around talking with mushers that we know and making new friends of mushers that we didn't know."

"For us, the ride itself was the best part. We loved being pulled by dogs that we knew. The tunnels and pedestrian bridges over traffic were fun. Cordova Hill is always exciting! It is always so nice to see all of the people lining the trail. They gave mushers and riders things like hot dogs, muffins, cookies, candy bars, water and even beer if you want it! Ed took a hot dog and a little ways down the trail we stopped and he fed a bite to each of the dogs. Vinnie and Lucas (in lead) got the biggest pieces!"

"Many of the people lining the trail held the list from the newspaper and would call out 'Good Luck Ed' or 'Go Michigan.' There were people sitting in lawn chairs, some in tent wind breaks, and playing instruments. The Buser boosters always have a banner strung across the trail that wishes Martin a good race." She saw signs for others, some well known, some not.

"The people all yelled words of encouragement. We always stop once to change the booties on the dogs. The 'trucked-in snow' had sand and gravel in it and that tears up the booties so they get holes in them quickly. Everyone seems to be in a good mood and the mushers ride their drag brake a lot to slow down their teams. The person riding the second sled gets whipped around the corners and usually goes over and drags or falls off," she adds with a laugh.

Having done the program so regularly, Nowak remembers the Idita-Rider meetings well, classifying them as a "nice but serious affair. As a rider you are checked into the meeting and given a packet of information. A couple of people that work for the ITC speak. One gal then goes through the packet explaining the information and answering questions. One sheet in the packet contains a drawing of where all the dog trucks will be parked so you know where to find them for the ceremonial start."

"When we get down there (4th Avenue) we have to check in with a certain volunteer so they know that we are there. At the meeting we get VIP passes which are on a lanyard. The pass is like a credit card with a picture of you and your musher (which was taken at the banquet) on the back. At the meeting they give do's and don'ts for riding the sled and waiting for the bus at Campbell airstrip."

"After the mandatory meeting is over, people are invited to go outside the Millennium where Dean Osmar usually has his dog truck, sleds, and dogs. He does a mini demonstration on how to act around the dogs and tells what the musher will be doing when harnessing the dogs. He demonstrates and takes his team back and forth so folks who have never even seen a dog sled will know what to expect."

Camera woman Donna Quante not only was an Idita-Rider, but made a movie of the experience. She first heard of the program via a brief story in the Travel Section of her hometown newspaper. She rode with Nils Hahn, who she won from the general pool. This means she didn't specifically bid on any musher, but as one of the winning bidders, she won a ride with him.

"It was an absolutely gorgeous day and I remember how very quiet it was out on the trail in the woods. I remember the muffin stop, too. That's where one of the dogs lifted its leg on a volunteer."

Georgia's Linda Birchall heard about the program her first year at the Iditarod: 1995. That was also the first year for riders. "I almost did it that year," she says, "but decided just to watch the start from the street, and see all the mushers."

"I became a rider in 2001," she continues, "because I always regretted that I didn't do it the first time! I wanted the experience of coming up the chute to the starting line, seeing the team all lined out ahead, and wanted to feel the thrill of the start, with all of its emotions and ceremony. I also wanted to see what it was like going down Cordova Hill."

She rode with Mike Nosko, whom she had met in 1995 when he was still dreaming about running the race. "I thought it was fitting to reconnect with Mike since I had my own Iditarod dreams, too: they just didn't involve running 1100 miles, more like 11," she laughs, referring to the distance riders got to ride at that point in time.

"Coming up the chute lived up to my dreams and expectations. The power of the team could be felt as the handlers struggled to hold them back. As we moved along up the street, the waves and good wishes from other mushers and volunteers made me feel part of the race in a very special way."

"I couldn't believe this little ol' Georgia gal was heading down 4th Avenue at the Start of the Iditarod. Wow! Cordova Hill was thrilling, of course, but my main memory is of being alone on a long stretch of trail with Mike and the dogs. It was heavily wooded. The sky was that deep, rich Alaskan blue, with hoarfrost on some of the trees sparkling in the midday sun. The soft shush of the runners on the snow, the gentle breathing of the dogs, and the wind in my face all combined in a symphony of sounds which spoke of peace, of joy, and of beauty. Mike and I chatted a bit, and then we would round a corner where a small group of spectators would be waiting, throwing candy bars and muffins, shouting encouragement to Mike and the dogs, and even greeting me."

"I heard a voice once, gently calling, 'Trail,' and we pulled over to let Dee Dee Jonrowe and her team go by. Then, we were alone again, just me, 'my' musher and 'our' team. I remember going under the tunnel, too, but I also remember one very sharp curve in the woods, by a creek, where other teams had experienced problems, even dumping some riders. Not Mike! He and his team took that curve so well that I was able to enjoy the magnificent scenery: wooden bridge, trees, sun-dappled snow in shades of pale blues and whites, and sparkling water with ice still floating on it in places. I can relive nearly every inch of that trail. I was sad to see the BLM buildings and my ride came to an end."

"Would I do it again? In a New York – make that an Alaska minute!"

Chapter 12

The Iditarod Family

Susan Butcher in Ruby.
Photo: Brenda Borden, www.duesouthphoto.com

"Susan."

Say just "Susan" to any Iditarod fan and they'll know exactly who you're referring to, four-time Iditarod Champion Susan Butcher. It's a status reserved for a few, such as Martin, Doug, Jeff, DeeDee, Rick, Aliy, Robert, and now Lance, the only musher to win both the Yukon Quest and Iditarod in the same year.

I wonder sometimes, however, if the mushers who've attained that first name recognition status really appreciate the depth of their reach. The extended Iditarod family is at once both widespread and closely knit. While they may fuss and even argue at times, when push comes to shove, the Iditarod Family is there.

When Tim Osmar broke his leg in several places during efforts to protect his family home from wildfires in the summer of 2007, friends, family and fans quickly came forward to help. It isn't just for mushers, either. When Lois Harter, a long time staff member of the Iditarod Trail Committee lost her home to fire, the fire crews hadn't even left her driveway when the news was going out on the Internet and friends and race fans were coming together to help; help for both eventually included an Internet auction to raise funds. As with Osmar, a bank account was set up to receive donations and the information on how to do so spread widely via Internet and word of mouth. The Iditarod Family does take care of its own.

There was no better illustration of this phenomenon of the Iditarod Family in action, however, than what came with the news that Susan Butcher had been diagnosed with Acute Myelogenous Leukemia. She was hospitalized in Seattle for treatment. The news came first in an email to mushers, and then quickly spread throughout the mushing community. By the end of the day, the Iditarod Family had swung into action.

One of the fun aspects of working checkpoints is the closeness you develop with those who return year after year. You get to know volunteers well. So it was no surprise to most when "The Tacoma Crew," as they're fondly known to Skwentna volunteers and race officials, was quickly busy making contacts and reaching out to help in Washington. It somehow came as no surprise to discover one of them had connections to the man most deeply involved in bone marrow treatment, nor that offers of help were coming from all over, not just Washington. That's what a family does, isn't it? Comes together to do what needs to be done.

Yet, the reach of the Iditarod Family goes far beyond this small, select group. By mid-week, posts to a variety of Internet groups were making the rounds, sharing the news and leading to more offers to help. It didn't matter whether your preferred breed was an energetic Beagle, fluffy, be-ribboned poodle, or tough working dog; the dog-related extensions of the Iditarod Family were pulling together on Susan's behalf. People from all points of the globe were going out to have their blood tested to see if they had a compatible tissue type with Susan. Some even signed up for the national data bank for bone marrow donors. They celebrated the announcement, when it came, that a near perfect donor had been found.

We're also discovering that within the family, there's a wide range of valuable knowledge to be shared. You learn that the recreational musher you hung out with is a physician's assistant and can share a wealth of knowledge on the disease and testing process. Another family member turns out to be a veteran of blood bank work, adding another piece to the puzzle. Another, who considered herself simply "a stay-at-home mom," lives in Washington and picked up the phone and called doctors at the cancer treatment center for some information directly from those who would know best.

Another Seattle Iditarod family member brought corporate experience to the task, trying to create some organization out of the flood of volunteers and requests for information. Others, even without such impressive backgrounds, were able to offer equally valuable services, ranging from offers to help with the children, run errands, or just provide a shoulder to lean on.

As we floundered about, thanks to the efforts of this world-wide extended family we share, order began to emerge from rushed chaos. Everyone pulled together.

Continuing with the Susan Butcher connection, later, when husband David Monson's bicycle was stolen from the hospital bike lot, the Iditarod family once again rallied. Although REI and the Seattle Bike Alliance quickly came together to replace the bike, race fans from all over offered money and support.

"Somehow it felt better to know that we were all sharing the outrage," said Jane Eagle.

It's a complex dance, but one that this same family has come together to do repeatedly under both relaxed and far more strained circumstances.

We are family.

Then came August 5, 2006.

The headline in the *Anchorage Daily News* read: *"Butcher loses cancer fight - IDITAROD LEGEND DIES: Four-time champion succumbs to leukemia at 51."*

Together, we wept.

Chapter 13

Sewing for the Iditarod: The Bootie Brigade

Lance Mackey, one of the first mushers to benefit from the services of the Bootie Brigade, stops to adjust a bootie during the start of Iditarod 2007.

Sixteen dogs.

Sixteen dogs with four feet each, each foot needing protection.

That adds up to 64 booties per Iditarod dog team.

Of course, that's just for one wearing. Booties, which are essentially a sock-like cloth covering for the dogs' feet with an adjustable elastic band at the top, have a tendency to get lost, have holes poked in them, or get wet, necessitating repeated changes along the 1,049 mile Iditarod Trail. Most mushers will use anywhere from 1500 to 2500 booties per race. At a minimum of a dollar a bootie, that adds up fast.

Enter the Bootie Brigade.

While many fans sew booties, this group of fans has come together to combine forces in an organized fashion. Their goal is to provide as many booties as possible each year to mushers in need by making them themselves.

Why do they do it?

"I make booties because this is a sport where-more than most-doing your best counts," says Tara Van Dyke. She explains. "The teams with the worst records in professional sports aren't applauded--the weakest players are traded and the coach is fired. With Iditarod, everyone is a winner, no matter what place they finish in."

Francine Dimmick echoes this sentiment. "Since I am unable to get to the Iditarod every year, this enables me to really keep in touch with the race even though I am thousands of miles away!"

"Making booties for the mushers is a way to become involved with the Iditarod," agrees Annie Myers, a long time race volunteer. Myers has arthritis in her hands. She's no longer able to cut out the booties for sewing, so other volunteers have done this part for her (and others), allowing her to complete the task. It's also allowed even those who don't sew to become actively involved. Team work is just as important here as on the trail.

The Bootie Brigade is headed by Rachel Curtis, a working mom who's never attended the race in person. She has, however, met and worked with a variety of mushers via the Internet in her quest to help coordinate the supply of volunteer made booties. One wonders, perusing the group's message board, if Curtis knew what she was letting herself in for when she started. She regularly deals with trying to figure out who has extra material or Velcro®, who needs more material or Velcro®, whether they need hook or stretch Velcro®, who can sew but not cut, who can cut but not sew, who can be called on for more booties at the last moment and a host of other issues.

"We average roughly twenty to thirty participants per year," says Curtis, "who come from all over."

It might also be noted that while it's cheaper to make booties than buy them, it isn't cheap either way. Postage alone is a tremendous expense. How do they do it?

To a large extent, they count on the good will of fans unable to sew. "We've gotten donations not only from around the United States, but from Canada and Australia," Curtis says. "In addition, some of the sewers purchase their own supplies." Many, of course, can't afford this expense and can only work out of the collected funds.

To help offset this expense, the group has formed a working relationship with Arrowhead Fabrics (AKA dogbooties.com), which has been beneficial for both. Arrowhead provides the materials needed at a cut rate and, in turn, the group buys all their materials from them.

"They've helped us over the years a great deal," acknowledges Rachel, who'd never made a bootie until beginning this group. Owner-Manager Louise Russell, of Arrowhead/Dogbooties.com, has provided them with not only the purchased materials but patterns and information, both to the group and in response to individual phone calls. Russell's ability to ask you how many booties you want and then tell you exactly what you need to complete the project saves many a headache.

Overall, the Bootie Brigade has provided over 35,000 booties to date. There are currently 116 members on its online email group, some of whom are individuals, others representatives for such groups as families, schools or various dog related clubs.

"We average 1000 booties per musher," notes Curtis, "although that number can also vary from year to year." Bottom line, it depends on the level of donations.

How many mushers have received Bootie Brigade booties?

That's a difficult question to answer. As the bootie seamstresses have gotten to know the mushers they're sewing for, many have developed a working friendship with them and want to help them out each year. Although that wasn't the intended goal, which was to focus strictly on rookies, it has somewhat changed the direction of the group.

It's also, in many ways, made it far more satisfying for those involved. True, some mushers are better than others at responding to emails and answering questions, but it gives the BB's, as they're known to many, a chance to get to know an Iditarod musher. Teachers and classrooms have gotten involved, too, with students writing messages of encouragement on each bootie that their donations have helped provide.

Jane Strayer is one of those involved in the classroom.

"I've made booties," she says. "My 6th grade students signed them prior to their being shipped to the mushers. One time, we knew to whom the booties would go, so the kids personalized them with messages, phrases such as 'Cold noses, warm toeses [sic]' and 'Run like the wind.'"

Her daughter signed a few booties with the phrase "Hoosier Hospitality." Imagine their surprise to get back one of those booties, now trail worn, after the race.

"I don't know how he kept it separated - I'm ruling out the lucky shot event - but it was obvious the bootie had been used. Much of the permanent marker was 'run off' by the dogs and there was even a doggie smell and a few dog hairs attached," recalls Strayer, laughing as she remembers her students' reaction to smelling a trail worn bootie.

Thus, although the master plan is always subject to modification, it's a win-win situation for everyone.

"Depending on our budget," says Curtis, "we try to help at least three to five mushers, but it varies." For instance, 6,857 booties were distributed between eight different mushers in 2007. They've extended this help to Junior Iditarod mushers in the past, too.

One thing that never changes is the difficulty of deciding who to help.

"Every year, there's been a waiting list of other mushers who have asked for help, too," sighs Curtis. "We are simply both physically and financially unable to assist everyone, unfortunately." As simple as booties may look to the average fan, it takes time and skill to sew them and shipping time must also be worked into the equation.

"Problems we have faced vary widely, but are usually centered on raising funds for materials, getting completed booties sent to the mushers in time to be packaged into drop bags, communication, having mushers withdraw prior to the race and not pass along their booties, size errors," that sort of thing, she says. "Most of these problems can be dealt with and rectified, however, and each year we get a little better and a little savvier."

Iditarod 2004 was one of the more disappointing years for Bootie Brigade members. Several of the mushers helped wound up having to withdraw prior to the race. While no one begrudged them the booties made and sent, it was still disappointing not to have their booties on the trail and imagine their progress up the trail.

No one can guarantee that all who enter will start the race, of course. Musher Frank Sihler's gracious move to pass along booties he'd received to Kelley Griffin, a Yukon Quest veteran but an Iditarod rookie, was applauded when he withdrew. As a result of Sihler's actions, booties made by the Bootie Brigade saw action not only on the Iditarod Trail but in the Yukon Quest, which Griffin ran, too.

"In 2006, instead of being sent to each individual musher, the booties were shipped to a central location to be distributed by a retired musher," notes Curtis. "In this way, we hoped that one final face to face discussion could take place to ensure that this musher really would be entering, and if not, if it's at all possible, that their booties would be passed along to someone else who needed them."

This is something group members have struggled with. Again, while no one begrudges the mushers who are unable to complete their quest to run the race, the goal is for everyone to be able to follow "their" booties up the trail. It makes it somehow more personal and makes it makes it easier to get volunteers and donations, bottom line, when those involved know they can "follow" their booties up the trail with a specific musher. It allows you to feel a part of the larger whole. It's also plain fun.

Randee McQueen, whose dog club became involved, agrees. "Our group is a dog club that also sleds. We started because of my niece's Girl Scout project and everyone has had so much fun that they look forward to it each year."

"There aren't too many sports where fans can directly contribute to the game," points out Tara Van Dyke. "I mean, the Green Bay Packers haven't called me up to sew them new uniforms!" she laughs. "So it is pretty cool that we can sew booties that actually run in the race that fans love so much."

Of course, it works both ways. The mushers are just as glad to be a part of it as the Bootie Brigade members are and it isn't just about the financial help.

Iditarod musher Bill Borden, one of the first to benefit from the then fledgling Bootie Brigade, summed it up best. "One of the best things about the Bootie Brigade and getting those booties delivered is in knowing that there are fans out there taking the time to care about what we are doing for the dogs and to have them participate with us in this great sport."

Borden, who is from Georgia and last ran in 2002, continues. "It's great to have fans stand at the start and cheer, but even better to know that there are fans aware of all the months of preparation it takes just for you just to get to the start makes it extra special."

"It truly is a blessing, sort of God's way of saying, 'Hey Musher, you and your family are not in this alone'."

Bill Borden holds up booties made by the Bootie Brigade.
The messages on them were provided by those who sewed.
Photo: Brenda Borden, www.duesouthphoto.com

For most, the musher banquet is a time
to renew old friendships and make new.

Chapter 14

The Musher Banquet

Hobo Jim

From the moment you enter the line outside and realize you're rubbing elbows with mushers, the musher banquet is a rush of impressions and experiences. You're surrounded by "suits," as well as those in heels and formal wear and clothing that indicates the wearer came straight from a kennel.

As you enter the Sullivan Arena, you hear the sounds of Hobo Jim playing live and look down on the sea of tables below, you realize, perhaps for the first time, how popular this event has become. There is seating for at least 1600 and no empty chairs. Yet, the arena is so large that one person's experience on one side or the middle may be totally different than that of, say, someone on the opposite side or the front or back. It's noisy, crowded and difficult to find faces in the crowd, but that, in an odd way, is part of the allure of the event. While looking for one person, you're likely to find someone else.

Your experience begins at your assigned table. Table assignments are largely random. You order a ticket and don't know where you'll be seated or with whom until you arrive. No matter. Discussion is difficult because of the noise, so everything tends to come in snippets. Sitting at a table, you'll find yourself trying to participate in three different conversations at one time, never quite grasping the entire thread of any of them, but still enjoying the moment. For many, this is their first encounter with the mushers. People are constantly moving and the buzz of conversation, barely interrupted by frequent announcements from the stage, pervades.

As I began to mill around, camera strung around my neck, I frequently found myself having to stop and step aside to let someone else pass. That's common. The tables are close and with coats hanging off the backs of most chairs, aisle space is tight. I note how many other cameras are in view, ranging from simple, single use cameras to the high tech camera sitting above the arena and manned by local and national news crews.

Walk down one side of the arena and you'll inevitably be buffeted by the lure of just one more souvenir. Remember, many of the guests have just arrived in Alaska, so this is their first opportunity to buy, buy, and buy. If you pause long enough, you're likely to go home with not just one, but another tee shirt – or two – and assorted buttons, pins, patches, books, or, well, "stuff."

Take the time to look around and you may feel the need to shake your head in disbelief. You'll find attendees in bibs and overalls right alongside those in fancy dress and heels, perhaps even fancy mukluks that have obviously never seen snow alongside kennel stained boots. Corporate banners line the walls above you, too, reminding you who helps pay for this show. Fur parkas are abundant, fur you just know has never seen the inside of a dog kennel. Mixed drinks share a table adorned with a white tablecloth and napkins, often alongside beer held by a souvenir glass donated by a sponsor. Some of these are instantly used, others tucked away as souvenirs as their owners head off in search of mushers or perhaps old friends they only see this one time a year.

Musher tables are scattered, ensuring you'll have to make several rounds of the arena to find those you seek, even with a seating chart in hand. At times it seems the ordering is so random as to have been made after tossing all the names into the air and placing mushers where their name lands. It's really not that bad, although just like the fans, the mushers don't tend to stay seated.

One of the unheralded perks of having to wander in search of autographs and photo opportunities is that you'll often find others of equal or even more interest. My first encounter with Martin Buser, for instance, took place on a stairway in the back as we both scanned the vast floor for familiar faces. From above, the floor of the arena is a sea of milling bodies, the only spotlight being on the small stage at the front.

Above the stage, video clips appear periodically on large screens. They range from promos for the *Iditarod Insider* to clips that remind us of those "out on the trail." This is the term applied by Iditarod faithful to those who've died.

After initial proceedings, most given over to thanking the sponsors and selected volunteers, the mushers are paged. It's finally their turn. They line up near the stage, chatting and joking amongst themselves despite frequent fan interruptions. They're called to the stage in the order they signed up.

After picking their numbers one-by-one and perhaps saying a few words, the mushers relinquish the stage to the next musher. As they exit, they're stopped to pose for an official photo just off the stage. And so it continues until all the mushers have picked.

That isn't the end. After their photo has been taken, mushers face a long line of fans seeking autographs and photos. It's tradition. Fans form a line off the stage where mushers exit. As they make that exit, mushers stop and sign whatever is put in front of them, no matter how long it takes. This is the fans' night.

And then, until Saturday, most mushers happily disappear from the spotlight, going back to their dogs, the real stars of the show.

Chapter 15

TGIF:
One Last Day of Deceptive Calm

Fans take one last chance to relax. From left, Betty Walden, Marlene
Daniels, Brenda Sperry, Jeannie Stinchcomb, and Julie Verrett.
Photo: Donna Quante, www.huskyproductions.net

The Friday before the ceremonial start is a deceptively
calm day. The musher banquet is over and most mushers
have largely disappeared from public view. Race volunteers

and officials are huddled behind closed doors dealing with final preparations. Fans are left to fill their hours with shopping or socializing with new and old friends. A book fair is being held.

Former wrestler, now musher-writer (*Wrestling the Iditarod*) Paul Ellering shares a moment at the book fair with Mike Dillingham, author of *Rivers: Diary of a Blind Alaskan Racing Sled Dog.*
Photo: Mary Dillingham

Don't let the air of calm fool you, though. There's nothing sedate about this day. A host of last minute details are being attended to out of public view, while upstairs, many gather to listen to the likes of Gary Paulsen and Mitch Seavey, as well as the Iditarod's chief vet, Stu Nelson. These presentations are part of the Winter Conference for teachers, but tickets are made available to the public.

Of course, speakers vary from year to year. The year after his Iditarod victory, Mitch Seavey spoke. Seavey is a different kind of speaker. He tends to be quiet, almost shy appearing, but provides food for thought. As an Iditarod Champion, you can rest assured that the audience members are listening carefully, hoping he might forget and drop some race strategy. Even those of us who have no real clue what we're talking about when it comes to competitive strategy like to think we have an inside angle, so this is fun.

Of course, that didn't happen, but it was an interesting, insightful presentation nevertheless. The entire Seavey Family has long been involved with the Historic Iditarod Trail development, a natural tie-in for educators. In addition, there was an intriguing link that year between Paulsen and Seavey. Paulsen, an avid reader and history buff, owns what was once the Seavey "B-Team," the one driven to Nome in 2005 by Tyrell Seavey.

Outside the doors of the conference room, of course, life goes on. Volunteers scurry around. Idita-Riders have their mandatory meeting. Fans are shopping at the merchandise tables. Officials meet. Children's questions pour into the Zuma email room. Mushers still around take the opportunity for one last relaxing moment in the lounge, smiling for photos and signing autographs, knowing human contact will be limited after this weekend. The dogs of the Iditarod are about to take center stage.

Joe Redington Sr. inspired the running of the Iditarod and is here commemorated at
Iditarod Headquarters, Wasilla. Seen from the back, showing Finisher's Patch.

Chapter 16

The Ceremonial Start

Noah Burmeister dogs
Photo: Jan DeNapoli, www.muzzysplace.net

The dogs.

You'll hear the dogs first.

As you make your way toward 4th Avenue to watch the start of Iditarod, you'll gradually become immersed in a cacophony of sounds and sights unique to the race.

Take a moment to ponder the history of this event as you approach. The history is far too broad to be covered by a quick summary. Let me just say it began with dreamers; two people who dared to dream of a race across Alaska, Joe

Redington Sr. and Dorothy Page. They were unlikely partners, Page a history buff, Redington an adventurer, but together they created an event synonymous with Alaska.

Unconsciously, your pace quickens as you near 4th Avenue. The sounds of the dogs, always the dogs, and a rising chorus of human voices begin to merge as you turn a corner and see the snowy street. Overnight, 4th Avenue has been transformed from one of downtown Anchorage's busiest streets to a compact, snowy trail leading the mushers out of town. The snow you're seeing has actually been stored for the occasion and then hauled in by a parade of dump trucks, which reverse the procedure after the start. It usually takes about the same amount of time to remove the snow that it'll take you to catch lunch afterward. The street is lined with webbed orange fencing to keep spectators back. Paper plates or hastily written signs with numbers tacked to the posts indicate which musher will be parked where. You never know who you'll see.

For a brief time on the morning of the start, anyone can get onto 4th Avenue and walk up and down the street, snapping photos, grabbing autographs, posing for photos under the start banner, or simply gawking. Just as with Mardi Gras, you can become a part of the show for a brief moment. This is prime viewing time for most and the street quickly becomes crowded. It's impossible to predict what your experience will be; just that it will be unique. Dog trucks line the streets, some sleek and shiny, others seemingly held together by that all-purpose tool, duct tape.

Dogs of all colors bounce about, some turning to take you in as you pass; others, perhaps the ol' pros in the bunch, cool and calm, rarely deigning to waste energy on fans. They come with a variety of names, many obvious, such as the spotted Spot, or flop-eared Floppy, but names can vary from ol' time rock'n'rollers to mushers' favorite foods, places, movie characters such as Lance Mackey's Zorro, or . . . well, just about anything, even cities such as Jeff King's Salem.

Lance Mackey's original version of a sit-down sled for the start.

Try to pull your attention from the dogs long enough to take in the variety of sleds on display. Since they'll be carrying an Idita-Rider for this part of the journey, many mushers use oversized sleds and add padding. Lance Mackey even jokingly added a cushioned seat one year for his Idita-Rider. These are the people who've paid to ride in the mushers' sleds, so they're catered to and many return year after year to experience the Iditarod in this unique way once again.

While most mushers won't have their race equipment in view today, if you're lucky you'll be able to catch a glimpse of a variety of snow hooks, sled designs, and even harnesses. Keep an eye out for "famous faces" strolling along the street with you, too, as it's not uncommon to find the likes of past champions in the crowd. Take advantage of this up-close opportunity because, almost before you know it, you'll find yourself being shooed off the street. The mushers need to start preparing.

Of course, for the mushers involved, the journey to Nome began long ago, with countless hours of training, endless miles of travel with their dog teams, and an intense focus on a dream that tends to exclude all but those who have gone before them. That's all behind them now as they gather on 4th Avenue. Look carefully, though, and you might catch a far-away look in their eyes as you speak to them, a look that tells you they're already out there, traveling the trail carved in ice and snow by so many others.

Beneath the start banner at 4th and D in Anchorage.

On paper, the concept behind the race seems outrageous. Take sixteen dogs, a sled, and cross wilderness Alaska in winter. No wonder many laughed at Redington and Page. As of 200, only 637 mushers have completed the race, a tribute to and symbol of the difficulty of the journey. More people have climbed Mount Everest than have finished the Iditarod. Yet, it's a journey made freely, even eagerly, and one that fans from around the world follow avidly.

Those who run the race are a mixed bag. There are doctors, lawyers, maybe even the proverbial Indian Chief. Native Alaskans are well represented anyway by the likes of soft-spoken John Baker of Kotzebue and Mike Williams, whose public campaign for alcohol awareness has become a focal point of his efforts to provide hope for others like him. Both Baker and Williams are extremely active with educational forces, as are many others, for that matter. Some are teachers themselves, such as 2006 rookie Bryan Bearss, most recently as a substitute, who viewed running the Iditarod as a means of testing himself as a teacher, this time as teacher-trainer of his dogs. Among the doctors on the runners in 2006 is Jim Lanier, a pathologist. Randy Cummings is another.

Libby Riddles, right, the first woman to win the Iditarod, rides to the staring line with Rachael Scdoris.
Photo: Mary Dillingham

Nearby, you might spy young Rachael Scdoris, who is legally blind, but determined to run the race. She first attempted it in 2005 and was forced to scratch due to sick dogs. In 2006, she ran with Yukon Quest champion Tim Osmar as her Visual Interpreter and finished. Up the street, you might find another Quest champion or two, such as Lance Mackey, Hans Gatt or Aliy Zirkle, the first woman to win the Quest.

Former professional wrestler Paul Ellering, whose professional wrestling name was "Precious Paul," has run the race and even written a book about it, *Wrestling the Iditarod*. 2006 rookie Kim Kittredge had climbed Denali, but faced an entirely different challenge "climbing" the Iditarod. 2007 rookie Bruce Linton is diabetic, making his rookie run all the more challenging as he's insulin dependent. Everyone has a story, which is part of the fun of following the race. Heck, if you looked closely, you might have noticed that one of the handlers for Martin Buser at the start in 2007 was none other than Alaska's "First Dude," Scott Palin, husband of Governor Sarah Palin.

One surprise to those expecting to see the first musher out parked closest to the starting line is that it's just the reverse. The first musher out will be parked up the street, way up the street, perhaps even on a side street. In order to allow an easy exit for the handlers and drivers of those whose musher has started, the lower bib numbers are actually parked the furthest away. That means, the last musher out has watched every other musher entered pass before they begin their short trek to the starting line. Just one of the ways the Iditarod Trail Committee organizes for efficiency.

Efficiency also demands that reluctantly, you'll be forced to leave the street as race time draws nigh. Even on this day, when most mushers are relaxed, routines dominate. Ganglines must be stretched out; dogs dropped and fed, some given random vet checks, equipment checked, decisions made. The media is usually hovering, too, perhaps hoping for a view of Jeff King's latest sled innovation. If so, they were surely disappointed. That would have to wait until tomorrow, when it's all for real.

Teams leave the starting line at two minute intervals. The mushers have been told their starting time and plan accordingly. Then, after the dogs are harnessed and the Idita-Rider tucked safely in their sled, they're moved up the street in an orderly, safe fashion. This requires teamwork between musher, handlers, and race officials. They're charged with moving entrants past fans, dog trucks, and other dog teams whose enthusiasm only adds to the mania that seems to grip teams as they progress ever closer to the starting line.

This is not a swift or steady trip to the start line. Remember, teams are going off at two minute intervals. The first to depart are the furthest from the starting line, so they've had to work their way through punchy snow, stopping and starting frequently. By the time they reach the line, the dogs are often wildly barking and leaping into the air, vocalizing their need to get moving.

Susan Butcher leading a team down 4th Avenue in 2001 after agreeing to take out an Idita-Rider.

Keep your eyes open, however, because this trend is changing. The success of Team Norway has created a move from the wildly careening dogs to a more orderly, controlled move, with dogs trained not to waste their energy needlessly. From an organizational standpoint, it makes sense, just as it does to the mushers involved. Try telling that to a run crazy husky, however. It's difficult for most to resist the excitement of the crowd.

The helicopters whirling overhead and the buzz of the thousands lining the way add to the "rush" of the Iditarod. Crowds do thin out on the street as the teams reach the line,

Are we ready yet?

with only designated handlers or associates of the musher actually going to the line with them. There, many mushers make one last trip up the line of dogs, stopping to scratch a few ears or whisper a word of encouragement to a nervous rookie. Then, the countdown begins.

Watch carefully. As the countdown nears blast-off, handlers step back, although all eyes are still trained on the dogs to forestall any tangles. Mushers might grab one last hug from family members or, if they've dallied visiting the team, even be sprinting back to jump on the runners as the countdown reaches . . .

3—2—1 . . . And they're off!

With that, the teams are away. The route will vary, depending upon conditions. Fans still line the streets, many offering tasty treats like donuts, muffins, or even hot dogs to passing mushers. Cameras click. One has to wonder what the dogs think of all this. Surely nothing in their training has prepared them for this rush of people, but most handle the pressure well. Some dogs are running only the ceremonial start, it might be noted, either for experience or perhaps as a last salute to an old-timer. Just as there are many reasons the mushers run, so, too, are there many reasons for the presence of each dog.

At the end of the run, teams come into a central point. Most recently, the ride has ended at Campbell Airstrip. After Idita-Riders are helped out of the sleds, volunteers guide teams to their dog trucks, each of which departed 4th Avenue right after their musher left in order to rendezvous in a timely fashion. Once at the trucks, mushers fall into their routine. Most will offer what might best be described as a kind of doggie soup to their teams, particularly if the weather is warm. They'll also carefully check over the dogs that ran. For the most part, fans won't view this operation, but it's an important one. An injury to a key dog during the start, which does not count for overall time, could create unforeseen problems. This is one reason many mushers don't run carefully pre-selected leaders during the start. They're too valuable to risk.

Of course, the Anchorage Start is just for fun. Sunday is the Restart, the real start of the Iditarod, whether in Wasilla or Willow.

Relaxing at the restart, 2007.

Chapter 17

The Restart and Beyond

The restart chute in Willow, 2007.

Time after time, handlers lead the dogs to the starting line. You can see some leaning back against the leads they've been handed to assist them in getting the Iditarod teams to the restart line. Others jog beside the teams, knowing the futility of trying to hold back a Nome bound team. Fans line the barrier fencing, cheering on favorites, perhaps wondering what it would be like to change places with those leading the teams, perhaps even ride the runners themselves someday. Officials are busy making sure everything comes off without a hitch, while volunteers line the chute and some, in fact, have already left for positions out along the trail. The Iditarod has begun, this time for real.

Ray Redington, Jr. at the 2007 Iditarod Restart.
He's walking through the musher parking and preparation area.

With their game faces on, the mushers tend to give off an air of being surrounded, maybe even protected, by invisible shields at the restart. Saturday was for show; today it's for real. Their attention has turned to making sure every last detail is taken care of and nothing is left to chance.

The scene at the restart mirrors that of Saturday, only with a new intensity. Hearing the sounds of a plane overhead, I have to ponder what all this must look like from the vantage point of an eagle. Perhaps like a sea of ants scurrying about, at first with no sense of order, then with order gradually emerging. For those on the ground, it's a rush of colors and sounds, with the barking of the dogs being the constant. It's a steady stream of quick snapshots, memories to file away.

Canadian Karen Ramstead's dog truck sports this license plate on the back.

Bright colorful dog trucks mingle with rusty, beat up looking trucks, each holding the dreams of the musher who owns it. Dogs of every color emerge from their boxes, somehow almost seeming to sense that this is the real thing. Sleds are checked and rechecked, then checked again. Snowmachiners rev their engines nearby, scooting across the lake as they await the start.

Along the chute, where orange fencing forms a barrier between fans and the first strides toward Nome these teams will take, fans line the fence, often several deep. The Willow route roughly takes mushers across the lake and after a slight turn, through a small residential area and then onto another lake trail. Volunteers struggle to keep order, often sneaking peeks at their favorites. Remember, volunteers are also fans.

Everywhere there are fans. They've come from near and far. Some wear their allegiance visibly, perhaps a musher tee shirt or cap, others seem to have opted for a mixed loyalty, a cap from one musher, a shirt from another, a button from a third. Some look more ready for an upscale party than a day on the cold ice, but most came dressed for comfort, not show. It's a burst of color and activity, with the mix of contrasting noises somehow blending into one sound, that of the dogs and the beginning of the race.

Just as with the start, each team approaches the restart line and waits for the countdown. As teams approach the line, family and friends, knowing this will be the last time they'll see their musher for some time, say their good-byes. You'll often see quick hugs for the youngest family members, those not quite sure what is happening, just that Mommy or Daddy seems to be leaving.

As teams head out, cameras capture the moment
as they cross Willow Lake in 2007.

While one has to believe that the mushers are glad to finally be out on the trail, for most, the restart goes by in a blur. Two friends, both volunteers, are headed to different checkpoints. This is their first experience as checkpoint volunteers. They're both excited and, well, a bit anxious. One is headed to McGrath, a hub of race action, and knows it'll be busy. He's nervous, but wouldn't give up this experience for the world. Iditarod badges strung around his neck, he's ready for the next step, the flight out. This is the spirit of the race, the willingness to go where you're needed and do what it takes, even when you're not quite sure what you're getting yourself into.

If all goes well, most teams will have passed through the checkpoints of Skwentna and Finger Lake by mid-day on Monday. The route alternates each year, the northern route for even numbered years and the southern route for odd numbered years. The most common question asked about this split in the trail is "Why?"

According the Iditarod Trail Committee's website, both sections of trail are a part of the Iditarod National Historical Trail, part of the array of trails to the gold fields. They were used for day to day travel to visit, bring in supplies, and deliver mail. Originally, however, only the northern trail was used for the race. The result was the smaller villages along that section of trail were heavily impacted by the race each year, putting both a financial and personal burden on villagers. In order to lessen the burden, the Iditarod Board of Directors decided to use both sections of trail, alternating annually.

"This decision had a three fold effect," says the ITC's website. "The northern villages of Ruby, Galena and Nulato only had to deal with the large group of mushers, press and volunteers every other year. The second effect was that the race was able to pass through the actual ghost town of Iditarod. Lastly, the villages of Shageluk, Anvik and Grayling were able to participate in the race."

In reality, few fans see the checkpoints in person. Travel to and from them is expensive and done at the whim of Mother Nature. Even the wife of a four-time race champion, Kathy Chapoton, wife of Martin Buser, wound up stranded in White Mountain in 2005 due to weather woes; so those yearning to fly the trail, beware.

The checkpoints closest to Anchorage, of course, see the highest fan traffic, but the race progresses so quickly now that visitors to, say, Finger Lake on a Monday afternoon are likely to miss all but the back of the pack. Volunteers at the Skwentna checkpoint will be cleaning up to await next year, while volunteers assigned to checkpoints further up the trail may not have even flown out of Anchorage yet.

Most fans watch this portion of the race, the largest part of it now, via cyberspace. The Iditarod web site updates race standings frequently, offering up photos and stories from the trail, as do many other sites. Internet email lists share the fun, emails flying through space as fans share their enthusiasm and any info they've been able to glean from other fans or race sites. It's a fun time for connected fans, one that allows those in faraway Norway, following their teams, to be just as connected as those in Alaska following local teams. The Iditarod truly has become an international event.

As the race winds down, of course, all eyes turn to Nome, an interesting place on its own. Built in an unlikely spot, regularly buffeted by winds and cold, even occasionally devastated by weather, it has survived despite the odds.

In many ways, little has changed in Nome since the time of the 1925 serum run. Close your eyes on the streets of Nome and you can almost feel the ghosts of the past. Leonhard Seppala lived here. Togo, Balto, and Fritz ran along these streets. Today, just as Togo stands watch at Iditarod Headquarters in Wasilla, Fritz now waits in Nome's museum for those who continue to live the dream.

Chapter 18

"Fan" is Short for Fanatic

An Iditarod collectible patch sewn to a jacket.

At some point in the Iditarod, everything begins to blur together. Endless days with minimal sleep are beginning to catch up to one and all. Fatigue has set in and one event blends into another as you frantically try to stay on schedule, groggily going through your list methodically, trying to make sense of it all. Hands once limber and pain free now throb from repeated actions, eyes are bleary, and the brain foggy. And, the race isn't halfway over!

I'm not talking about the mushers, by the way. I'm talking about the avid fans, those who climb out of warm beds in the middle of the night to catch updates, click obsessively on the link, trying to make sense of how names once absent from the top rankings are now competing for a spot in the Top Ten. I'm talking about fans who have compiled a master list of "must check" Internet sites; fans that form little cliques of equally obsessed friends and debate each and every event as if their lives depended on it. These are the fans of the Iditarod.

Iditarod fans are a special breed. They come from all over the world, many paying thousands of dollars to attend the race in person or giving up hard earned leave time in order to have the "fun" of volunteering along the trail in -55 degree weather. Some pay up to $7500 to ride in a musher's sled at the start, joining the elite group known as Idita-Riders. Many return year after year, riding with the same musher or branching out so as to get to know other mushers in a more personal way than mere fandom allows.

You'll see them in the lobby of the Millennium Alaskan Hotel in Anchorage, browsing past the Iditarod merchandise table "just one more time." Surely, they think, I've missed something. There must be one more thing here that I absolutely must buy. Already decked out in their Iditarod sweatshirt and wearing Iditarod patches on their coats, they don't even stand out in the crowd. We all look like that. True, the design on the shirt may differ, but it's almost an Iditarod ritual to find the perfect shirt each year and, well, browse until your wallet is empty. Been there, done that; what can I say?

Those unable to attend in person can still follow along. Idita-parties were common on start and restart day, ranging from places as unlikely as Atlanta, Georgia, to Los Angeles,

California. Even more impressive, the Atlanta contingent was hosted by a genuine Iditarod musher, 2002 finisher Bill Borden. Kathy Mattes, an admitted wannabe, hosted a California gathering, while in Pennsylvania, Donna Quante, producer of the video "Pretty Sled Dogs," about Canadian musher Karen Ramstead, hosted a group with the assistance of her own husky crew. Yep, Idita-mania can be celebrated near and far.

Even those unable to find a gathering close enough to attend weren't left out in the cold, pun intended. The Internet brings fans from all over the world together. Email brings them even closer. They zip emails back and forth with a pace at which any sled dog would be proud.

Early on, a conversation might have run something like this:

"Gould."

"Are you sure it isn't Zirkle?"

"What happened to Martin?"

"They lost Martin?"

"Look at Lance go!"

"Wow, how did Jeff get up there so fast?"

"Did you read Tyrell's story?"

"Did you watch the video?"

"What video?"

"Who's ahead?"

"Larry's cool."

"Huh? Who's Larry?"

"Did you . . ."

Fingers clicking, every possibility is exhausted until they fall into bed, wrists sore, tired, only to be compelled to rise in a few hours to begin the cycle all over again.

It might go something like this as the mushers enter Nome:

"Someone's coming!"

"Who?"

"Oh, drat, the page won't open!"

"What page?"
"Who is it?"
"I don't see anything."
"Is it him?"
"How cold is it?"
"I love the helicopter shots!"
"Him who?"
"The video isn't loading!"
"Why am I seeing NASA?"
"I can't get the update!"
"How do I save it?"
"Who is it?"
"Quick! Right click!!!"

Disjointed conversations like this are the norm, not the exception, for those who can only follow the Iditarod via computer. From the moment the mushers prepare to leave Anchorage, no, actually long before, faithful fans and the merely curious tag along via cyberspace.

For those who can't drop everything and fly to Alaska to follow the race in person, this is the next best thing. In recent years, there's been a proliferation of web sites dedicated to the Iditarod. More recently, several chat rooms and internet groups have been created to serve the purpose of bringing fans together to share their enthusiasm and knowledge. As a result, comments such as the above tend to fly through cyberspace at a pace almost too fast to take in. Dozens, sometimes hundreds participate and the shared experience can be a frustrating but fun one.

The starting point for most is the Iditarod's web site. Whereas fans were once reconciled to hours, if not days between updates, they now expect updates regularly and quickly. A musher just crossed the line in Nome? They expect to see it live. As far as many are concerned, if it isn't reflected on the updates almost instantly or available live, it is cause for alarm. We've been spoiled by the speed of cyberspace. Never mind that the web-master might actually be outside watching the event. We want info and we want it NOW.

Idita-Support has members from around the world.
Patch design: Bonnie Lundberg

Email has brought people together from around the world and has made distance irrelevant. As a result, try to imagine an email with a Scottish lilt intermixed with a Texas twang or Southern or Norwegian accent and you've got a taste for what it might be like to share the race with friends from around the world.

Perhaps the most amazing thing about this phenomenon, however, is that most often these friends are people you've never met in person and, in fact, are unlikely to ever meet. It doesn't matter. The shared interest is all it takes to pull them together. Toss in, hopefully, someone willing and able to maintain some order out of the enthusiastic chaos resulting from hundreds of exchanges, not all coming through in as timely a fashion as they should, and you can find yourself on the sidelines watching the race through the eyes of the world.

For example, prior to the existence of Iditarod Insider, an Alaska based fan shared the arrival of Team Norway's Robert Sörlie in Nome in 2005 as it happened on her television screen. The event was televised in Alaska and it was described around the world by email as it happened.

Another fan shared experiences of what it had been like when the teams passed through Skwentna, an early checkpoint. Others posted from Nome. Perhaps more amazingly, the mushers themselves even occasionally find time to "phone home" and the word is spread via email. You no longer have to be there to know what's happening.

Even without "inside sources," so to speak, it's still possible to follow the race quite successfully simply by surfing the net. More and more mushers have a website and it isn't just the ones belonging to the big names that are worthy of viewing, either. In 2007, for instance, rookie Heather Siirtola's website was a great source for those trying to find information on those at the back of the pack. Siirtola's father was in Nome and updated the site as quickly as news was received. For those who've long mourned the lack of coverage for those bringing up the rear, his efforts were much appreciated. With his daughter entered in Iditarod 2008, he plans to be doing the same once more.

In between checking the standings on the Iditarod site and Team Norway, many fans stop by Cabela's talk forum to discuss race strategy or simply strike up a conversation. As the race wore down, far from being fixated on the race, some chatters were more concerned about finding a way to stay in touch with those they'd met at the cyber corner of Cabela's and Iditarod Trail. It's all part of being a part of the Iditarod Family.

Cabela's Iditarod site boasts the insightful writing of musher-writer Jon Little. Since not everyone has purchased access to *Iditarod Insider*, his descriptive words fill a void. He's found himself weathered in and riding on the back of a snow machine more than a few times in order to move on up the trail, but no matter what the year, his stories quickly became the topics of emails flying through cyberspace. Amazingly, Little even finds time to reply to a few of them himself.

Again, that's the fun of cyberspace. You just never know who'll drop into the room. Much to the delight of fans in 2006, Little found time to share a personal moment, the birth of son Salem Little. The littlest Little impacted his father's race coverage by arriving two weeks early, forcing Little to make a rushed trip home from Nome, where he was covering the conclusion of the race, but few begrudged him this early exit.

Besides Cabela's site, as noted, many mushers maintain their own web sites. Links are usually available on the Iditarod site via the musher bios or musher list. True, some are more active than others. Some seem stuck in 2003; others start out strongly but fade as the race progresses. Others have a slick, professional look. There are countless intriguing sites out there, too many to list them all, such as Ed Stielstra's journal, which features comments from wife Tasha, a musher herself, during the race.

Of course, the websites belonging to the big names attract the most attention. Sometimes those manning the home fort in cyberspace even become stories.

Kathy Chapoton, wife of Martin Buser, had no intentions of becoming a part of the Iditarod story in 2005. All she was doing was following her husband up the trail and sending reports back for Martin's website. Well, she was *trying* to follow him up the trail. Flying with Paul Claus, father of Iditarod musher Ellie Claus, she found herself grounded in White Mountain. As it turned out, the checkpoint's crew was also grounded, unfortunately in Nome.

Chapoton and Claus were put to work. Paul Claus helped check the dogs to help determine whether to drop or continue on with the individual dogs, while Chapoton quickly became White Mountain's "mother hen," as race winner Robert Sörlie characterized her.

Her eventual report that appeared on the Buser web site blends into the stories told by others. What emerges after reading them all was the impression that she most likely had little time to give her own husband more than a peck on the cheek and instructions where to park. That's a part of the Iditarod. Do what you need to do.

That's what makes this race so much fun to follow in cyberspace. Stories like the one swirling around Chapoton may make headlines in the paper the next day because of her status as the spouse of a race champion, but there are countless other stories out there waiting to be discovered. All it takes is a bit of exploring in cyberspace to find them.

For instance, Tasha Stielstra reported that race officials in Kaltag asked her husband Ed to carry a packet of dog meds to Unalakleet for vets there. Thus, history repeated itself in a fashion, only this time it with a sled dog team carrying medicines up the trail for other sled dogs.

It's stories like this that makes the race so special. Simply by clicking around in cyberspace, you can stumble on such gems.

*At race time, to locate personal musher websites, go to www.iditarod.com and click on the list of mushers. Then click on individual musher names and check their biographies to discover available websites.

Chapter 19

Why Be a Fan?

"Since the race chatter has died down and the mushers are getting home, getting rested and trying to answer mail," Georgia's Linda Birchall told members of an email list of which she's a member, "I thought a 'love letter' to ALL the mushers was appropriate."

Birchall went on to provide a bit of her own background and explain, perhaps to herself as well as the hundreds of others on the list, why she follows the Iditarod so faithfully. Her interest in the Iditarod began "with a combination of admiration, awe and wonder one Saturday afternoon in 1985," remembers Linda. "I was watching *ABC Wide World of Sports* and they showed Libby Riddles battling that awful snowstorm to persevere and triumph as the first woman to win the Iditarod."

"I was amazed!" she says. "My interest grew and although information was scarce here in Atlanta, I eventually found the Trail Committee and have been an ITC member since the early '90s." She holds a lifetime membership in the organization.

Birchall attended her first Iditarod in 1995. By that time, animal rights activists had targeted the race and as lawyer, she was determined to investigate in person.

She was also curious. "I wanted to try to get some understanding about what would make people take a team of dogs across 1,049 miles of wilderness in the dead of winter."

Business brought others to the race. Bill and Brenda Borden, also from Georgia, went to their first Iditarod in 1998. They had established a business relationship with one of the mushers and their son Jordan was to be an Idita-rider that year. That was just the beginning of their love affair with the race, one that went far deeper than it did with most fans.

"The mushing fever was contagious," says Brenda Borden, who owns Checkpoint Mortgage with her husband Bill. "The people we met were all so nice and the dogs were just awesome, so we found ourselves going back the next couple years as volunteers." It all seemed innocent enough at that point.

"Then Bill decided he was going to run the race!"

Their lives haven't been the same since. They spent two and a half years acquiring a team and trainers, training, running qualifying races and then participating in the Iditarod in 2002. In the process, they bought a condo in Alaska and quickly became involved in many of the organizations they participated in at home in Georgia, such as Rotary. Bill ran the race with a team of dogs acquired from veteran musher Lynda Plettner, finishing near the back of the pack but finishing.

While some might have been able to turn their backs on the race and resume their "normal" life, that wasn't going to work for the Bordens. Although family and business obligations have kept Bill off the runners since his first and only run, it was addictive.

"We still follow the race and report back to our web site," said Brenda. "There comes a point when you're fully caught up in it. Even when we're unable to follow the race in person, we are still following it online and posting photos from other Idita-fans that are too busy having fun!" In prior years the Bordens have followed the race all the way to Nome by plane, reporting back.

The dogs, of course, were the draw for Bill and Brenda. Unable to turn his back on his team, Bill spent a considerable amount of money buying the team from Plettner. Some are still running with other mushers, while others have been re-homed, including one goofy blonde named Hazel that now lives with me. In addition, they now host a sort of mini-Iditarod kennel at their home in Georgia, where a once pristine lawn has given way to the antics of five lively retired sled dogs.

Bill also speaks to various groups regularly about the race and what it has meant to him and others. He's usually accompanied by one of the retired dogs. His willingness to give back to the sport is a huge part of what draws others to this race.

The accessibility of the mushers is what astonishes new fans. I have to admit, when I attended my first race in 2000, I might have expected to meet a few mushers, after all, I did have some connections, but I hardly expected to find myself sitting beside them in the hotel lounge or at a table. Most are more than happy to strike up a conversation, sign autographs or pose for photos. Mushers Karen Ramstead and Bill Pinkham shared our table one year while Joe Runyan and others sat nearby, as did race champion Doug Swingley and wife Melanie Shirilla. This aspect of the sport surprised Linda Birchall, too.

Iditarod Champion Dick Mackey, who ran in the first Iditarod, poses with Mary Dillingham and Helen Hegener at Iditarod Headquarters. Mackey is father to Rick and Lance Mackey, also Iditarod Champions.

"My admiration grew and continues to grow because these mushers give of themselves and take time with their fans," she explains. "That first trip, made before I really knew anyone, I was still able to get photos with DeeDee, Martin, Jeff, Rick Swenson, Rick Mackey, etc. They actually talked to me!" she laughs. It's a feeling many fans share.

Linda's experience goes further, however. She was able to visit the kennel of then wannabe musher Mike Nosko. Much to her surprise, he invited her to return the next day to ride the runners herself. She was invited back over the next several trips she made.

"He shared the most precious commodity he had with me, his time."

"I've never been invited to Tiger Woods' house, or Greg Maddox or Lindsey Davenport's. I've never sat at the kitchen table and shared a roast beef sandwich with Michael Jordan or Dan Marino. I've never gotten a phone call or a letter from Kristi Yamaguchi. I never got to go out and work with Jeff Gordon's pit crew. Did you ever receive a used baseball from Derek Jeter? How about a wrist band from Pete Sampras? Or maybe a golf tee or ballmarker from Tiger Woods? Of course not! But I did get some booties from Jeff King and a feedbag or two. I have been lucky enough to be up close and personal with mushers."

Linda goes on to explain. "Nowadays, so many of our sports 'heroes' are nothing more than overpaid egomaniacs, who are only interested in themselves. Not so with these mushers, most of whom are down-to-earth, friendly, approachable 'folks' and I, for one, appreciate that and admire them all the more." This is a trait most fans admire and respect, knowing the mushers don't have to take the time to rub elbows with them at the annual Musher Sign-up/Volunteer Picnic in June. Yet, they're there, like multiple champions Martin Buser and Jeff King who attended the 2004 picnic even though they wouldn't sign up until later.

It's this sort of behavior, going the extra mile, which fans appreciate. "As long as that continues," agreed Linda, "they will always have the most loyal, dedicated and die-hard fans in the world -- people like us, who can't stop talking about them and their sport year-round."

Of course, it isn't only the mushers who are the draw. For many, it's simply a chance to renew old friendships and make new ones. I've often joked myself that the race is a real distraction to all the socializing I try to cram into a few short days, and Colorado volunteer Brenda Sperry seems to share that sentiment.

"As the day wore on," she says, remembering her first day in Alaska, "I met more and more past Iditarod friends, and as the days and weeks wore on, yet more. As I said before, this is why I keep coming back, year after year." Brenda has taken her love of the dogs to another level, entering school to earn a degree in what is dubbed "vet tech," a skill that will serve her well in future Iditarod races as a volunteer.

For Maureen Morgan, the spouse of Iditarod veteran Bob Morgan, it was the dogs, too. "Watching those teams churn up snow and show their power, tongues to the side, smiling faces and 'whoosh' as they passed by . . . it trapped my heart." For the Morgans, one dog quickly snowballed into 72 and Bob would eventually run the race three times.

Rachel Curtis, of Illinois, remembers reading Jack London's *The Call of the Wild* in junior high. "I've been a fan for years," she says, "and honestly can't even remember when I started liking the Iditarod and the sport of mushing. It possibly started with reading *The Call of the Wild* back in junior high school. I read a lot, and if I like a topic, I'll read more about it." Rachel has never attended the race in person but follows it avidly on the Internet as many others do.

Also like many, she has found a way to be involved from a distance. Rachel has headed up the Bootie Brigade (See Chapter 13), a group of supporters that has sewn booties for mushers in an effort to repay some of their kindness. She oversees a Retired Sled Dog web site and has helped place several retired sled dogs in new homes. She has also spoken to several different grade schools over the last few years about mushing, booties, and the Iditarod. Like the mushers, she's trying to give back to the sport she so enjoys.

Why?

Because she remembers the kindnesses of the mushers. "The mushers are almost all extremely friendly, polite, and go out of their way to thank you for any help you offer, whether it is monetary support, booties, or other items."

For Linda Birchall, the mushers also "exemplify the American spirit. I'm convinced that the Yukon Quest and the Iditarod are the last true wilderness-pioneering events in the world," she says.

The one thing all the fans I contacted kept coming back to, however, was the availability and willingness of the mushers to let us be a part of their world. While most fans will never visit Alaska, let alone run the race, they have an opportunity to experience it through supporting those who do live the adventure.

"I am so grateful that they let us "armchair mushers" share their dreams," declares Jane Eagle. "In our imaginations, we run sled dogs across the tundra and through the forests, along the Yukon, to a burled arch and a lit lantern shining through a cold arctic night. Every one of them carries our dreams and our prayers for them in their sled bags. What an amazing bunch of people!"

The Nugget Inn sits alongside the finish line in Nome.

Chapter 20

Nome: Where Dreams Come True

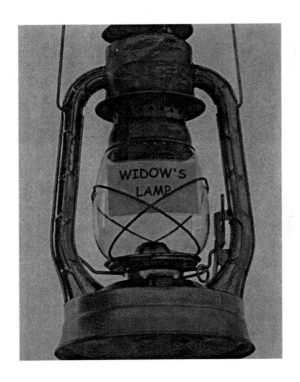

"The Iditarod is over! Lance Mackey has won!"

This comment, almost a direct quote from an Anchorage based news station in 2007, shocked me. Unlike NASCAR, the Iditarod doesn't end once the first musher passes under the Burled Arch. Each musher continues on, finishing only when they and their team pass under the arch themselves.

Despite this, as far as many were concerned, Lance Mackey's victory in 2007 was the end of the Iditarod. Talk forums that were once beehives of activity were slowing down. Fans were saying their goodbyes and promising to meet, "same time, same place" next year. Even the most rabid of fans was perhaps not refreshing one of the Nome cams as often in hopes of seeing a musher finishing under the arch. Yes, for some, the race was over.

Despite this, the race wasn't over. Not only were mushers still on the trail, but there was work to be done even when all were safely in Nome, a city of less than four thousand clinging to the icy shores of the Bering Sea.

Nome is, in itself, an experience alien to most fans. Few will travel here and, in fact, several years passed before I made that journey.

When I first arrived in Nome in March 2004, already fatigued and half sick, Nome was another world to me, a far cry from the tidy, compact world of the Iditarod in Anchorage. Instead of being able to walk out a door and into the dog lot, the dog lot was a long, cold walk down a shadowy street. Instead of a free shuttle bus downtown, everything in Nome was seemingly a (then) $3.00 taxi ride away.

Iditarod Headquarters, Nome

Iditarod HQ Nome would have practically fit into the Redington Ballroom at the Millennium Alaskan Hotel in Anchorage. The body heat generated by a full crowd inside was enough to send even those of us seeking warmth quickly back outside. The command center was largely one room, one that shared space with boxes for musher mail and any assorted items left behind for pickup. A couple of computers and phones on 2-3 tables made up the communications center, with a few more for media and mushers in the larger room. Cell phones without Nome connections are often largely useless as anything other than paper weights. People only a phone call away in Anchorage have to be physically tracked down for answers, assistance, or simply words of wisdom in Nome.

Most of us made do with foot power, trucking from hotel rooms and apartments at all hours of the day and night, often alone, something most of us would never do in the "real world." We headed out, shivering beneath our layers of clothing, only to break out in a sweat as we moved indoors once again. Fat Freddie's became something of the social center of what essentially became a sort of small, self centered universe. The 'real world' seemed far, far away.

Unlike Anchorage, the volunteer numbers had tended to dwindle by the time the race reached Nome in 2004. Trail vets and volunteers were enduring a nasty virus on the trail but continued to do their job. No warm hotel room for the dog lot crew. Instead, they huddled in a cold, airy cargo container used for storage.

The view from behind the arch as a team finishes.

Dogs came in and came in and came in. Iditarod 2004 was the year of the Idita-Detour and flights out of Nome were somehow affected by this fact. Flights were shuffled and canceled at the whim of the weather. Dogs were everywhere in the dog lot. Dogs in front of you. Dogs behind you. Dogs to the left and dogs to the right. Dogs on the hillside. Dogs at the dog lot entrance. Dropped dogs in a tent. Dogs in front yards nearby. Dogs everywhere you looked.

Even more importantly, as those first few flights failed to leave, dogs began to back up. Dogs that normally would have been flown home almost immediately after a finish were not, meaning new spots to park later arrivals had to be found. The Finishers' Banquet came and went. As the days passed, some mushers, having tried repeatedly to get out with their dogs, wore a far wearier look than their trail adventures could account for. It was one worn by fans and volunteers unable to get out, too, some of whom slept in the airport that year. Yet, despite it all, what needed to get done, got done.

The burled arch in storage, not far from where it stands during the race.

Yes, it's obvious to those in Nome that the race isn't over until the last musher arrives. Front Street remains partially blocked by that big pile of snow with the arch firmly planted in it. The arch remains until the last musher has arrived. Residents of Nome simply drive around it, perhaps not as thrilled to see it still standing as those who don't live there might be, of course.

They're remarkably indulgent. They smiled as those of us new to Nome scrambled (okay, fell) down steep banks of snow to cavort in the "Nome National Forest," a collection of discarded Christmas trees firmly planted in the ice. They smiled as we coaxed them to take our picture with some of the revelers involved in Nome's St. Patrick's Day Parade. I mean, after all, one does go to the finish of the Iditarod expecting to parade down the street with green haired wannabe-Irishmen, right? They even smiled when we darted across streets in front of them, perhaps knowing, "This too shall pass."

For the Iditarod Trail Committee, of course, it isn't over until not just every musher is into Nome, but all their dogs and gear have been cared for and transported to an off-season resting place, too. By then, everyone is tired beyond imagination, yet there's still work to be done. Even in normal years, it isn't unusual for dogs to remain in the dog lot after most mushers have departed. Someone has to take care of these dogs. The person doing that is a volunteer. No, the race isn't over.

Crated and ready to fly home.

Somewhere, as the race winds down, with the back of the pack still on the trail, hard working, extremely fatigued Nome volunteers keep an eye on those dogs, making sure each team will be ready to leave on schedule, just as they did the day before and the day before that. Just as they will tomorrow and the next few days for the stragglers. Somewhere, a vet remains on call, just in case, and someone else begins what will be a massive clean-up task in the dog lot. Even the most well- intentioned mushers tend to drop everything in the rush to load their dogs to leave and it all has to be cleaned up.

Out on the trail, the same clean-up is going on in different places, of course, while White Mountain and Safety still wait for the last musher to go through. Homesick or not, volunteers there will still provide the last musher with the same courteous welcome and care. Vets will check the dogs; volunteers will direct the musher to a parking area and show them where fresh straw is located. Nothing changes. The race isn't over.

True, the chute banners and arch will eventually disappear, but there are banners and posters to be taken down all over town and stowed for next year, hotel rooms to be cleaned, and heaps of used straw and dog waste to be disposed of. No, for some, the Iditarod isn't quite over.

You'd think at this point most would cease to care. Yet, although it sounds absurd, it was somehow reassuring to have someone holler at me across the dog lot when I went through the area. How easy it would have been for the one on duty to shrug and ignore that distant, unidentified person strolling into the dog lot. But, she didn't and wasn't satisfied until I identified myself. After all, the dogs need to rest and unauthorized visitors aren't allowed.

Even more amazing, she was actually concerned I'd be offended. Instead, I thanked her, noting that any musher worth their salt should be happy she was taking such good care of their dogs. I might note that it didn't seem to matter what time of day or night it was, either, someone was there.

It was the same this year. It will be the same next year. They're there when one team leaves and there when another arrives. They're there to help you load dogs into the trucks to leave. They'll be there to lend you a hand climbing into the back of the truck for your ride to the airport with your dogs. They're not going anywhere quite yet. They still have a job to do, long after the spotlights have been turned off. That's the sort of people you have overseeing this race.

From just behind the Burled Arch, looking
down the street that mushers come up to finish.

So, before you say good-bye to the Iditarod too soon, pause a moment. For many, even with the winner and top twenty into Nome, the race continues. Even with final clean ups and details being planned or attended to, dogs and gear being unloaded at home and attended to, planning is underway for the next race.

Somewhere, mushers are dreaming.

In these dreams, Happy River is just that, a happy, painless experience. There are no broken sleds in these dreams, no sick dogs. There are no sleds hanging from, go figure, a snow hook stuck in a tree as Aaron Burmeister spoke of at the 2004 Red Lantern banquet; no duct tape helping hold your sled together, no tree stumps jumping out to surprise you.

These are the dreams of a dog musher, dreams of running a fine team of dogs across the Alaskan wilderness alone, Northern Lights dancing above, the Burled Arch on Front Street waiting to welcome you.

Lance Mackey and Larry celebrate at the Nome Banquet, 2007.
Photo: Brenda Borden, www.duesouthphoto.com

Gary Paulsen, 2007

Afterword

Gary Paulsen: "It's Like a Dance"

My first Iditarod was in 2000. I had come up to attend the Iditarod's Teacher Workshop, then in its infancy. One of my most distinct memories was of Diane Johnson, that year's Teacher on the Trail, speaking about a hatchet she'd been given. She eloquently connected it to *Hatchet*, a book on survival despite the odds by Gary Paulsen.

Like me, not to mention countless others, Gary Paulsen's *Woodsong* was our introduction to the race. We credit Gary Paulson with changing our lives forever. At that point, however, I'm inclined to say neither Diane, who's become a friend, nor I, had any genuine dreams of ever meeting Gary Paulsen in person. It just seemed too much to hope for. That changed.

My first encounter with Gary Paulsen was when I interviewed him for the Iditarod's web site. Despite my occasional air of "been there, done that" approach to talking to mushers, I have to admit to a certain amount of giddiness at the opportunity to talk to Gary on the phone. Meeting him in person, of course, was an extra perk.

Later, as silly as it sounds, it was a real rush to hear myself being hailed at the 2005 restart and turn around and see it was Gary calling my name. He was just about to fly out to Skwentna with musher – pilot Rick Horstmann but took the time to yell to me to stop and chat. I say this not to make myself seem important, simply to indicate how down to earth Gary Paulsen is. I'm proud to say I consider him a friend. He's someone I'd like to sit around a campfire with someday and just listen to stories he's spun.

He did just that the day before the race started, albeit in the Millennium Alaskan Hotel without the campfire. It didn't matter. The teachers and race fans there were spellbound. Gary Paulsen is a natural storyteller and it showed.

Gary opened his reminiscences by reviewing his life. Although it's well known that his childhood wasn't good, reading it and hearing it from his own mouth are two different things.

"That library card with my name was the first time I had an identification of my own," he recalls. He'd slipped into the local library to warm up and been befriended by the town librarian. Unfortunately, he can't remember the name of the book he walked out of the library with that day but admits that it was probably an easy reading type because he wasn't a good reader at the time. He says he would read a few pages and have to go back and reread them to take it all in. He noted that even today he doesn't read authors, he reads stories.

Of course, the simple action of getting a library card didn't magically transform his life. He was still living the life of a child of alcoholics and enduring all that comes with that. He joined the army "50 years ago this year (2005)" and took a job in the fledgling aerospace industry soon after his discharge. He was involved in the launch of the first spy satellite tracking station.

"Out of the blue one night," he remembers, "I decided that I was going to write." He packed his company car and drove it to California where he promptly left it. He began applying for jobs in writing and jokes that his resume of the time was "my first piece of fiction." Those familiar with his tale know he was given a chance to write but perhaps not how much he got caught up in the Hollywood lifestyle.

"I didn't drink all the way through the army," he notes. "I'd seen what it did to my family." Yet, for reasons perhaps even he can't understand, Gary Paulsen fell in with the crowd surrounding the likes of actor Dennis Hopper and didn't write for ages. He did drink, however. "It was bad. Very bad," he states flatly.

May 5, 1973, was a momentous day for him. It's the day he quit drinking. He openly admits that he's a recovering alcoholic and regularly attends Alcoholics Anonymous meetings twice a week. At the time, he was deeply in debt and signed a contract to write two books. Legal problems abounded. In an effort to sort out his affairs, he hired some lawyers who got the money, not him.

He fled to the wilderness. By now, he had a wife and a young son. They moved into a lean-to in Minnesota with a barrel stove for heat. He was once again, or perhaps it'd be more accurate to say *still* in debt. He was forty years old.

In order to survive, he began running a trapline on foot. Minnesota had passed a law saying it was illegal to use a four wheeler in the situation he found himself in, so he had no other option. That is, until a neighbor, a sprint musher, gave him a broken down old sled and four trapline dogs. Unfortunately, none were leaders. As a result, he found himself still walking, only this time with a rope tied around his waist, acting as lead dog. However, his life was about to change.

"I met a guy who gave me a sick dog," he remembers, a faraway look sneaking into his eyes. "He didn't think she was going to live but it turned out that she just had worms." This dog was Cookie. Paulsen still carries her photo in his wallet.

Cookie started out in wheel position and slowly worked her way up to leader. From that point on, Gary Paulsen never looked back. There's almost a wistful look in his eye as he remembers one vivid moment etched in his memory forever. It involved a full moon above the silently running dogs and a steam rising from them and almost crystallizing in the air, blocking his view of the dogs.

"It was the most beautiful thing I've ever seen. It was like a dance," his term for the fine bond that forms between man and dogs. In fact, he wanted to relive that moment so much that as he approached home, he simply turned the team and disappeared into the wilderness with them for a week. No one knew where he was and he didn't care. He'd fallen in love with the dogs.

One day, he told some friends, "I think I'll run the Iditarod." He shakes his head. "I had no clue."

He also had no money and only the beginnings of a team. Much to his surprise, the community rallied around him and he suddenly found himself a musher with sponsors, but one with no dog team, which he accumulated gradually. A neighbor gave him a '60 Chevy truck, the same one characterized in his book *Winterdance,* to use as a dog truck.

"I used cafeteria trays for the floorboard," he recalls, "and one door was tied on with a bungee." The door fell off when they untied it. The trip from Minnesota to Alaska took eight days.

Somehow, against all odds, Gary Paulsen, without having ever run a sled dog race in his life, was about to run the Iditarod. At that time, you didn't have to qualify to run the race. Instead, you had to find someone who would sign that you were capable. Paulsen obtained his signatures and soon found himself in downtown Anchorage at the Iditarod starting line.

"Cookie thought I was insane," remembers Paulsen, recalling the noise and confusion. "So, I had a dog named Wilson that I decided to put into lead." Laughing at his own naivety, Paulsen recalls the teams ahead of him charge down the street and turn right. He even acknowledges telling Wilson to watch. "Wilson watched every one of those teams intently," he laughs, "watching them go down the street and turn right." Paulsen got a big laugh from the teachers as he described his theory that surely Wilson would figure it all out by observing how the others did it.

It didn't work. "Wilson took off like a rocket and instead of turning right, took us right through the crowd." The team charged on through back streets and yards as Paulsen wildly tried to find something, anything solid, to set a snow hook in. He quickly discovered that street signs and car bumpers didn't make good anchors and became totally lost.

"Do you know how embarrassing it is, wearing your Iditarod bib number, to have to ask someone, 'Which way to the Iditarod?'"

Those who've read *Woodsong* or *Winterdance* will recall that this race was not an easy one for Paulsen. At one point, he found himself in the middle of nowhere about to repeat his pattern of walking away from things when they got bad.

"I was frustrated and walked away from the team. I must have gone a hundred yards before I turned around. I knew I couldn't do it alone. I went back and talked with Cookie. 'You've got to do it,' I told her. She did."

Now true, being not just a sled dog but a leader, Cookie still had many lessons to teach her human. Paulsen recalls seeing tracks going into water and insisting that Cookie lead the team through it, for instance. After telling him in every way she could that this was not a good idea, she gave in and lead the team through, emerging in a pout, stomping her wet feet as only a sled dog ticked at the stupidity of its human can, then bit him on the knee. Later, Paulsen discovered only one other team had taken this path. The rest had gone around. Had he listened to Cookie, he would have stayed dry and his knee intact.

Paulsen went on to become an Iditarod finisher, but his mushing career was brief. He began suffering chest pains and was told to give up stressful activities. He called one of his musher friends, Mark Nordman, currently Race Manager for the Iditarod, from the doctor's office to go get the dogs, knowing he'd find it impossible to part with them if he waited.

"There was suddenly an eighteen hour hole in my day." The energy he'd given to running dogs fueled his writing and he has since become one of the most prolific authors around, his work spanning all age groups.

Iditarod fans, of course, know him from *Woodsong* and *Winterdance* but the book he's most proud of is *Nightjohn*, which began life when he started to research a series of slave chronicles in order to write a book on Sally Hemmings' relationship with Thomas Jefferson.

As for his return to mushing, Paulsen says it began with a simple phone call. He was asked if he'd like to come up and sign some books during an event known as the Ikidarod. As the day wore on and organizers prepared to go home, he was asked another question, the one that ultimately brought him back to Alaska: "You wanna take a spin?" asked an organizer, waving at their own sled.

"I knew I was had," he laughs. Although his plans to run Iditarod 2005 didn't pan out because of problems getting quality miles on the dogs – not to mention some interesting confrontations with moose that must have been auditioning for roles in his next book – Paulsen says he's here to stay, reaffirming his determination to run the Iditarod again and perhaps even the Yukon Quest. Sadly, he was forced to scratch early in Iditarod 2006 due to an injury and unable to run in 2007 due to family matters, but is entered for 2008.

Diane Johnson with Gary Paulsen

As I stood at the front of the room taking notes, I watched the Iditarod's now Education Director, Diane Johnson as she watched Gary. She clutched the hatchet in her hand. She would have him autograph it after he spoke, bringing her full cycle. Just as it had happened with me, the words of Gary Paulsen had brought her to Alaska. Like Gary, Diane now runs dogs. Like Gary, I now write.

"Oh, great, another life I've ruined," joked Gary as I tried to verbalize it to him later. It's a sentiment he's obviously heard often.

Thanks for ruining my life, Gary. I wouldn't have it any other way.

Printed in the United States
87283LV00003B/301-429/A